SELF RELIANCE: THE STORY OF RALPH WALDO EMERSON

SELF RELIANCE: THE STORY OF RALPH WALDO EMERSON

PEGGY CARAVANTES

MORGAN REYNOLDS PUBLISHING

WORLD WRITERS

Robert Frost

Stephen King

Jane Austen

Charles Dickens

Ralph Ellison

O'Henry

Roald Dahl

Jonathan Swift

Leo Tolstoy

Zora Neale Hurston

Mark Twain

Mary Shelley

C.S. Lewis

Ralph Waldo Emerson

Self Reliance: The Story of Ralph Waldo Emerson
Copyright © 2011 by Morgan Reynolds Publishing

For more information write:
Morgan Reynolds Publishing, Inc.
620 South Elm Street, Suite 387
Greensboro, North Carolina 27406

Library of Congress Cataloging-in-Publication Data

Caravantes, Peggy, 1935-
    Self Reliance : The Story of Ralph Waldo Emerson / by
Peggy Caravantes. — 1st ed.
        p. cm. — (World writers)
Includes bibliographical references and index.
    ISBN 978-1-59935-124-7
    1. Emerson, Ralph Waldo, 1803-1882--Juvenile litera-
ture. 2. Authors, American--19th century--Biography--Juvenile
literature. I. Title.
    PS1631.C339 2010
    814'.3 — [B 22]
                                    2010008143

Printed in the United States of America
First Edition

To my granddaughter Katie,
with love and congratulations
upon her graduation

TABLE OF CONTENTS

CHAPTER ONE

FAMILY TIES

T HE MEN IN THE EMERSON FAMILY were
expected to be ministers. It had been that way
for six generations. Ministering was the family
trade and as a young man growing up in Boston, Ralph Waldo
Emerson never dreamed he would pursue any career other than
the ministry. So, in January 1829, at the age of twenty-five, he
was ordained as a minister in the Unitarian Church, fulfilling
his and his family's expectations. But eventually his ideas and
beliefs would lead him to resign his pulpit. In the process, he
would establish himself as one of the most influential writers
and thinkers in the United States.

Ralph Waldo Emerson. An 1876 engraving from an original drawing by Sam W. Rowse

Ralph Waldo Emerson was born on May 25, 1803, to Ruth Haskins and the Reverend William Emerson. The name "Ralph" came from his mother's youngest brother, Ralph Haskins, a merchant seaman whom she had helped raise. "Waldo" came from Rebecca Waldo, his great-great-grandmother on his father's side. He was born in the wooden parsonage of the First Church of Boston at the corner of Chauncy Place off Summer Street. First Church, also known as the Old Brick, was the oldest church in Boston, founded by the Puritans in the seventeenth century. Although he traveled a great deal in his life, Emerson never lived far from this neighborhood with its lovely gardens, orchards, and open pastures.

Ralph was one of eight children and rated only a brief note in his busy father's diary the day he was born: "Mr. Puffer preached his Election Sermon to great acceptance. This day also, whilst I was at dinner at Governor Strong's, my son Ralph Waldo was born. Mrs. E. well. Club at Mr. Adams.'"

Ralph Waldo Emerson's family. Emerson is the older man in the back, center, next to Lidian, his wife.

William and Ruth Emerson were strict parents, determined to make sure their children worked hard and knew the difference between right and wrong. Their sons were not allowed to play in the streets near their home for fear they might meet "rude" boys. Instead, Ralph stood "at the gate in a state of pleasing excitement half fear half hope that the 'rude boys' would come near enough for him to see them!"

Though limited to his own yard, young Ralph took an interest in all of the activities that occurred near the parsonage, which was located in a neighborhood of stately Lombardy poplars and splendid orchards. At nearby Boston Common, cows and sheep grazed at a community pasture. The Common was also where townspeople gathered for festivals and other events, including public hangings. One festival was a mock-Indian "Feast of the Squantum." Next door to the parsonage was an orchard of St. Michael pears, which tempted young Ralph greatly. "I remember sitting . . . and wishing for some of those pears," he later recalled.

Ralph grew up in the early days of the American democracy, as the country began to develop politically and to move westward. Boston was a small provincial town in the early nineteenth century, with little more than 25,000 residents, but it was growing and becoming more prosperous as a center of trade.

Ohio became the seventeenth state the year that Ralph was born, and that same year two explorers, Meriwether Lewis and William Clark, set out to explore the territory between St. Louis, Missouri, and the Pacific Ocean. In Massachusetts, the Middlesex Canal had opened—the first canal built for commercial use in the young nation. Considered an engineering marvel, the twenty-seven mile canal connected the Merrimack River to the port of Boston, opening up the vast interior of New England to merchant trade.

"When I was a boy I used to go to the wharves," Ralph later recalled, "and pick up shells out of the sand which vessels had brought as ballast, and also plenty of stones, gypsum, which I had discovered would be luminous when I rubbed two bits together in a dark closet, to my great wonder."

Another memory of the water was not so pleasant. When he was six years old, he suffered a skin problem, perhaps eczema, that his father treated by making him bathe in the ocean. Ralph hated the baths, largely because of his fear of the deep water. His father, determined to carry out the treatment recommended by a doctor, tossed his son into the waters. Although Ralph choked and gasped, he did not scream. However, he never forgave his father for what he considered a cruel action. Forty years later, he still recalled the man "who twice or thrice put me in mortal terror by forcing me into the salt water off some wharf or bathing house, and . . . the fright with which, after some of this salt experience, I heard his voice one day . . . summoning us to a new bath, and I vainly endeavoring to hide myself."

A typical day in the Emerson household began with a simple breakfast, prayers, and recitation of Bible verses by every family member. After that, their mother went to her room to meditate. The children knew not to disturb her. Each day also had its own special routine. For example, Thursday was the day when their father could bring a guest, perhaps a fellow minister, to dinner. Three days a week, the children had hot chocolate and plain

An 1854 engraving of Boston Bay

toast for breakfast. The Saturday meal always consisted of salt fish, vegetables, melted butter, and pork scraps.

The Sabbath began on Saturday evening. At that time, all work ceased and the family did not go anywhere or have any visitors. The children put away their toys and laid out their Sunday clothes. The next day, everyone went to church to attend Sunday school and to hear their father preach at two services. They spent the rest of the day quietly until a full twenty-four hours had elapsed since the Sabbath began.

Ralph started attending a Dame School when he was three years old. Women taught such schools in their homes, emphasizing reading and writing. Ralph did not make enough progress that first year to please his father, who wrote to a friend: "Ralph does not read very well yet."

In 1807, when Ralph was four, his brother John Clarke died, most likely of tuberculosis. John Clarke was eight years old, and his death devastated the family. In a letter to her sister, Ruth Emerson wrote, "I feel daily the agonizing pain arising from his loss."

The following year Reverend Emerson's health began to decline. While preparing for a Sunday service, he was overcome by intense pain, brought on by a severe hemorrhage of the lungs. He recovered, and for a while, resumed his day-to-day activities, which were many.

The clergy stood at the top of the social ladder in Reverend Emerson's day, and he was pastor of Boston's oldest and most prestigious church. He also founded the Boston Philosophical Society, organized the Massachusetts Historical Society, and helped found both the *Christian Monitor* and the Anthology Club. The Anthology Club published the *Monthly Anthology*, of which William Emerson was the editor, and established the only library of substance in Boston open to the public.

William Emerson wrote for other publications as well and lectured. In 1808 he published *A Selection of Psalm and Hymns*. Reverend Emerson also spent a significant amount of his time and income, which was twenty-five dollars a week, thirty cords of wood a year, and the use of the parsonage house, on books.

Blond with blue eyes and sandy hair, William Emerson stood nearly six feet tall and was known as a dignified, genteel, and honest man who "expressed himself decidedly and emphatically, but never bluntly or vulgarly." Born in 1769, he had graduated from Harvard College in 1789, and tried to break the chain of becoming a preacher, preferring to become a merchant or lawyer. But his mother's wishes and tears prevailed. He served as minister in the town of Harvard in 1792, and in 1799 became minister of First Church.

Though well-liked by parishioners of First Church, William Emerson spent more time on his book collection, the local historical society, and the establishment of the library than on his church duties. A minister friend said of him, "in his theological views perhaps he went farther on the liberal side than most of his brethren with whom he was associated. He was, however, perfectly tolerant toward those who differed from him most widely."

By 1810 William Emerson began to show signs of tuberculosis, and his doctors advised him to go to Maine for a vacation. However, he worried about money, because he had not managed to save any of his earnings. He was working on a book about all of the pastors who preceded him at First Church, hoping it would supplement his income, but in the meantime, he had little to provide for his wife and children. "Our family," he wrote to his sister Mary Moody Emerson, "have so long been in the habit of trusting Providence, that none of them ever seriously thought of providing a terrestrial maintenance for themselves and their households."

By February 1811, William Emerson was too ill to welcome his sixth child, Mary Caroline, into the world. However, as soon as she was baptized on April 7, he departed for Portland, Maine. William Emerson never saw his family again, dying on May 12 at the age of forty-two from a lung hemorrhage and a blockage in his stomach caused by a tumor.

His body was returned for the funeral to Boston, where he was interred in the King's Chapel burying ground. Because he had been chaplain of the Ancient & Honourable Artillery Company of Boston, its members and sixty coaches preceded his

hearse to the cemetery. His two oldest sons, William and Ralph, followed the hearse, on foot.

All Reverend Emerson left his family was a collection of books, which Ruth Emerson immediately sold to help provide for herself and six children. The oldest, William, who was ten when his father died, tried to share the responsibility of caring for his siblings—Ralph Waldo, eight; Edward Bliss, six; Robert Bulkeley, four; Charles three; and an infant sister, Mary Caroline. The parish agreed to give a five hundred dollar annual stipend to the Emerson family for seven years after the minister's death and allowed them to continue living in its parsonage for one year, although they actually ended up staying three years.

Ruth sent her son Robert Bulkeley, who had a mental disability, to live with relatives in Maine. To keep the rest of the family together until the older boys could help out, Ruth Emerson took in boarders. She had only two goals: to help the family survive and to educate her sons. Despite the hardships she faced, Ruth Emerson remained serene, devout, sweet, and even-tempered. The pastor who succeeded her husband at First Church described her: "Her mind and her character were of a superior order, and they set their stamp upon manners of peculiar softness and natural grace and quiet dignity. Her sensible and kindly speech was always as good as the best instruction; and her smile, though it was always ready, was a reward."

Still, Ruth Emerson needed help with her large family. Assistance came from her husband's sister, Mary—a fiercely independent, outspoken woman who never married and whose "rude speech" and eccentric ways "sooner or later offended even those who recognized her great worth."

Mary had frequently visited the Emerson household, and two years before his final illness, William Emerson wrote to

Concord, Massachusetts. Minute Man National Park

his sister, asking her to return, permanently: "Your residence in my family until death or matrimony separates us is necessary to my happiness."

Mary Emerson returned, and stayed at the parsonage for almost a year after her brother's death. This was an important time in Ralph's rapidly changing life. To him, Mary was a "kind aunt, whose cares instructed my youth." Years later, he would recite her "high counsel" to his own children: "Lift your aims;" "Scorn trifles;" "Always do what you are afraid to do;" and "Sublimity of character must come from sublimity of motive."

In time, though, Mary Emerson became restless at the parsonage and left for Concord, Massachusetts, a village some twenty miles northwest of Boston. Leaving her brother's family did not prevent her from continuing to be the boys' Puritan conscience. When not with them in person, she kept up an active correspondence, correcting their beliefs and their behavior.

Mary Emerson took great pride in her family lineage and ancestors, and she made sure that her nephews respected their heritage as well, understanding that the Emerson legacy set them apart. One of Ralph's childhood friends recalled that the Emerson boys grew up convinced that they "had a peculiar proud carriage of the head, a hereditary trait." Ralph, in particular, the friend wrote, "always put and kept a distance between himself and others."

The boys' education was a primary goal for both Ruth Emerson and Aunt Mary. Ralph attended a public grammar school for several years, then entered the Boston Public Latin School in the fall of 1812. Like the other boys, he dressed in a coat and pants made of blue nankeen—a long-wearing cheap Chinese cotton cloth brought to the United States. The school's purpose was to prepare boys for college but Ralph was a mediocre student. He was more interested in books not included in the curriculum than those that were, and he often complained about "tomorrow's merciless lesson."

The school's original buildings were torn down when Ralph first began attending, and classes met in a series

An illustration of a traditional boys' school in the 1800s that would have been similar to the one Emerson attended

The Old Manse was built in 1770 by the Reverend William Emerson, Ralph Waldo Emerson's grandfather. In 1842, the American writer Nathaniel Hawthorne rented the Old Manse for $100 a year. Friend Henry David Thoreau planted a vegetable garden for the Emersons here.

of temporary places until the new school was completed. The school had no money for regular desks, so the boys sat on long, thick, hard boards. William Bigelow, the headmaster, spent a good amount of his time drinking alcohol and frequently lost his temper when students answered incorrectly; wrong answers were met with a strike from his cane.

Fortunately for Ralph, the youngest class of students got to leave Bigelow from eleven to twelve o'clock each day to go to a special school, where they studied writing and arithmetic. Walking to the other school each day, Ralph was often tempted to skip classes and play on the Common, even though he

This is an ink and watercolor drawing of the ruins of the U.S. Capitol following British attempts to burn the building. It shows fire damage to the Senate and House wings, the damaged colonnade in the House of Representatives shored up with firewood to prevent its collapse, and the shell of the rotunda with the facade and roof missing. The artist is George Munger, ca. 1814.

knew the consequences were that he would be "punished for it by imprisonment [at home] on bread and water." Ralph learned to write acceptably and to do enough arithmetic to get by. But he would struggle with math throughout the remainder of his schooling and life.

By this time, the United States was engaged in a war with England. The War of 1812 was fought under the motto "free trade and sailor's rights." It began because of British violations of American shipping rights. Relations between Great Britain and the United States had often been strained following the American Revolution.

Although Boston residents knew about the war and the battles at sea—such as the one when the USS *Constitution* defeated the HMS *Guerriére*—they had not been directly affected until sugar, coffee, tea, cotton, and other goods became scarce and expensive. When flour rose to seventeen dollars a barrel, Ruth Emerson started thinking about leaving Boston. Ralph's step-grandfather, Ezra Ripley, invited the family to come stay with him in Concord at the parsonage, later called the Old Manse. Ripley had married William Emerson's widowed mother and became pastor at First Parish in Concord.

While Ruth tried to make a decision about leaving Boston, the British were threatening to invade Boston Harbor and to send soldiers into the city from the surrounding towns they controlled. Benjamin Gould, the new headmaster at the Boston Public School, ferried students to Noddle Island in the harbor to fill sandbags and to construct barricades. About the same time, Ralph's only sister, three-year-old Mary Caroline, died. Ralph had enjoyed pulling the pretty little girl in her wagon, and was devastated by the loss.

In August 1814, the British attacked Washington, D.C., capturing the navy yard and burning the White House and the Capitol. Only a tremendous rain storm saved the rest of the city. A few months later, Ruth decided to accept Ezra Ripley's invitation to move to Concord. The family left Boston.

JAN 14 1913

A. WILLIAMS & CO.
RAIL ROAD
& TOWNSHIP MAP
OF
MASSACHUSETTS
Published at the
BOSTON MAP STORE,
283 Washington St.
1879.

1. CAMBRIDGEPORT.
2. EAST CAMBRIDGE.
3. CHARLESTOWN.
4. EAST BOSTON.
5. SOUTH BOSTON.

Lith. by J. Mayer & Co. No. 4 State St.

CHAPTER TWO

A DEVELOPING MIND

I N CONCORD, Ralph began attending the Concord grammar school, where his excellent memory allowed him to learn long literary passages that he loved to deliver to adults. One day, as Ralph and his uncle Samuel Ripley walked through the village, his uncle noticed that all the adults they passed spoke kindly to Ralph. The younger boys, on the other hand, made remarks, tried to knock his hat off, or shoved him.

His uncle asked him: "How is it, Ralph, that all the boys dislike you and quarrel with you, whilst the grown people are fond of you?" The question surprised Ralph, who did not believe that the other boys disliked him. He thought they just teased him because of his quiet humor and his lack of interest in their slapstick jokes and noisy fun. One day, however, as the boys taunted him about his refusal to join in their games and sports, the harassment erupted into a fight. Ralph's step-grandfather, Ezra Ripley, talked to all of the boys, but when he asked Ralph for his version of the story, Ralph became tongue-tied and said nothing. When his Aunt Mary heard about his failure to speak up, she scolded him sharply: "Fie on you! You should have talked about your thumbs or your toes only to say something."

On Monday, February 13, 1815, Concord residents received the news that England had signed a peace treaty with the U.S., ending the war that had begun in 1812. Ralph wrote to his older brother, William, who was at Harvard College: "A smile was on every face, and joy in every heart."

With the war over, Ruth Emerson moved her children back to Boston. They stayed with members of her family for a few months, with Ruth serving as their housekeeper in exchange for room and board. In the fall, Daniel Parker, a Boston merchant, needed to make a trip to London and offered Ruth the use of his Beacon Street house rent free if she would serve as housekeeper to his family. Ezra Ripley let the Emersons borrow a cow in order to have milk for the children. Ralph's job was to lead the cow to nearby pastures every day.

In the fall, twelve-year-old Ralph and his younger brother Edward returned to the Boston Latin School. For three days a week, they also attended a private school to study French, a language in which Ralph excelled. Before long he was reading stories in

French. He did not like his Greek and Latin studies, though, and was glad when the time spent with them was cut to allow the boys to study geography.

The Boston winter of 1816 was especially hard on the Emersons. Ralph and Edward had to share one coat, so that on really cold days, only one of the boys could attend school. Worse than the cold was the taunting of the other children about whose turn it was to wear the coat. William helped out financially during vacations from Harvard by teaching at his uncle Samuel Ripley's school in Waltham, Massachusetts. Well-meaning friends assisted Ruth and her sons through gifts such as fabric, cheese, sugar, tea, and small amounts of cash.

Because all the boys attending the Boston Latin School would go to college, they were considered an elite group of students. Therefore, President James Monroe paid special attention to them when he traveled to Boston in 1817 as part of his national tour to restore harmony between the nation's political parties. The school stationed the boys by the gun house on the Common so that they would be easily visible to the president. They all wore uniforms of blue coats and white pants with an artificial red and white rose stuck in their buttonhole. The honor guards waited impatiently for hours. As Monroe finally rode by, he bowed to the boys, who took off their hats and cheered the president.

Shortly after the event, Ralph concluded his fifth and final year at the Latin School. He finished with only average grades and did not receive any of the scholarship medals. However, he was well-read because of his interest in books not included in the curriculum. He later admitted that "the regular course of studies, the years of academic and professional education have not yielded me better facts than some idle books under the bench at the Latin School."

In August, Ralph passed the Harvard entrance exams unconditionally. He entered Harvard at the age of fourteen, which was not unusual for that time, as most boys entered college at thirteen or fourteen. Still, his early acceptance added to the family's financial woes. Like his brother William, Ralph received the Penn legacy scholarship that came from a bequest by an elder in First Church. However, the family still had to find money for other expenses not covered by the scholarship.

The university president, John Thornton Kirkland, had been a friend of Ralph's father, and he took a special interest in Ralph. He named him freshman messenger, a position that paid Ralph's tuition and dormitory rent. This meant that Ralph lived in the room immediately below the president's office in Wadsworth House. When President Kirkland wanted Ralph's assistance, he simply tapped on the floor. Ralph's duties included carrying messages to the students, posting notices, running errands, and helping to enforce the forty pages of rules that every student had to obey.

The rules included required attendance twice a day at prayers, church attendance on Sundays and other special occasions, strict observance of the Sabbath, adherence to a dress code, and permission to check out from the library only books on the approved list for underclassmen. Failure to obey the rules resulted in fines or other disciplinary actions. To further help with his expenses, Ralph served as a waiter in the Junior Commons and tutored President Kirkland's twelve-year-old nephew.

The curriculum, which involved mostly memorizing and reciting, disappointed Ralph. As in the Boston Latin School, he struggled with mathematics. When his Boston Latin School teacher, Benjamin Gould, heard about Ralph's poor performance, he came to Harvard, as Emerson later recalled, "to give me advice of my sins or deficiencies in mathematics, in which I was then, as I am now, a hopeless dunce." But by that time, Ralph had decided that it was not "necessary to understand Mathematicks & Greek thoroughly, to be a good, useful, or even great man." Ralph enjoyed history, especially the study of people, and his favorite activity was public speaking.

When vacation time came, Ralph taught at his uncle Samuel Ripley's school, where older brother William also had taught. Ralph, not yet fifteen years old, taught fourteen students. At the end of the session, Samuel Ripley bought him a new overcoat. Ralph would rather have had the money to give to his mother. He wrote to brother William: "It appears to me the happiest earthly moment my most sanguine hopes can picture, if it should ever arrive, to have a home, comfortable and pleasant, to offer to mother; in some feeble degree to repay her for the cares and woes and inconveniences she has so often been subject to on our account alone."

Because of the strict rules and the lack of any organized games or sports at Harvard, the dormitory students often rebelled with disorderly behavior. Food fights in the dining hall, dumping buckets of water on people from open windows or in stairwells, and throwing stones at windows were all common. When Ralph began his sophomore year, freed from his freshman position under the strict guidance of President Kirkland, he began to participate more in the other boys' activities.

One Sunday night, a food fight broke out between the freshmen and sophomores. A dining hall monitor summoned the president, who rushed over to stop the fight. Kirkland suspended four sophomores whom he considered the main ringleaders. In protest, all of the sophomores gathered at the Rebellion Tree, a campus elm where on the eve of the War of Independence American soldiers had rallied.

Kirkland responded with more suspensions, resulting in the entire sophomore class walking out. Ralph, along with others, broke a twig off the Rebellion Tree and promised not to return to classes until the president reinstated the suspended students. Three weeks passed with neither side relenting. When twenty-seven of the students finally petitioned to return, Ralph was among that group. He participated in other activities, but never as a leader, and learned when to back off to avoid disciplinary action. Near the end of his sophomore year, the Pythologian Club invited him to join their organization. Ralph immediately told his brother William that membership marked him as "one of the fifteen smartest fellows" at Harvard. The club's purpose was serious reading and extemporaneous discussion of all kinds of topics.

After his sophomore year, Ralph again taught at his uncle's school in Waltham, enduring long days with the boys until they finished their homework at around 8 p.m. Ralph's junior year was an important one. He returned to school with a lighter heart because he did not have to worry about his financial situation. William had established the School for Young Ladies in a room of his mother's home in Boston. The girls' tuition payments covered the family's expenses, and Ralph no longer had to help support his younger brothers. Upon arrival at Harvard in the fall, Ralph decided that he wanted to be called Waldo, the name that he would prefer the rest of his life.

Even more important to his later career as a writer was his decision in January 1820 to keep a journal, which he called *Wide World*. In the journal, Emerson wrote his thoughts on all subjects. He also recorded ideas and quotations of other people, books he had read, and books he hoped to read. This and subsequent journals became a literary bank from which he drew ideas for lectures, essays, sermons, and poems.

The instruction during his last years at Harvard was much better than his first two years, which included a lot of memorization and recitation. The college hired professors to teach instead of relying solely on tutors. Two of the new instructors were Edward Everett and George Ticknor; both had earned doctorates at one of Germany's leading schools, the University of Gottingen. They brought to Harvard some of the intellectual freedom they had enjoyed in Europe. Their first change was to switch from student recitation to formal lectures. Emerson and his classmates were awed by the men's polished deliveries and their challenge to the students to become independent thinkers.

However, the professor who most influenced Emerson was Edward Tyrrel Channing, a twenty-eight-year-old lawyer and editor of the *North American Review*. The younger brother of a famous Boston Unitarian preacher, William Ellery Channing, Edward Channing had joined the Harvard faculty in 1819 as a professor of oratory. His first speech to the Harvard students was about the power and importance of the orator. He immediately captured the attention of Emerson, who always enjoyed public speaking. Channing's main theme was that the oratorical style must fit the times as well as the speaker's own style. The orator also should tailor his own topic to his country rather than emulate famous orators from other countries.

Channing stressed a quiet delivery; short, simple sentences, and honesty to put conviction behind the speaker's words. Such traits would one day characterize Emerson's simple, sincere, and natural lectures. Channing, along with Everett, created in students "the classic New England diction—the measured, dignified speech, careful enunciation, precise choice of words, and well-modulated voice" that for many years marked young men as Harvard graduates. Channing also stressed writing. He helped Emerson prepare an essay for the Bowdoin Prize in Emerson's junior year, for which Waldo won second place and a cash prize of twenty dollars. By the time Emerson was a senior, he submitted weekly essays to Channing, who helped polish his writing skills.

Despite his close relationship to the young professor, Emerson did not improve his overall scholarship. In an October 25 journal entry during his senior year, he wrote: "I find myself often idle, vagrant, stupid, & hollow. This is somewhat appalling & if I do not discipline myself with diligent care I shall suffer severely from remorse & the sense of inferiority hereafter. . . . I need excitement."

He found some of that excitement in a chemistry course during the second semester. This interest in science became the foundation of his later philosophy about nature and man's relationship to it. But the course that most deeply influenced him that spring was one on moral philosophy. Professor Levi Frisbie taught that man had an intuitive moral faculty, enabling him to distinguish between right and wrong. Although Emerson did not know it at the time, his acceptance of Frisbie's teaching was preparing him for his own later views about how man gains insight on moral issues.

Commencement at Harvard was such an important community event that it became a state holiday with businesses and banks closed. The activities on August 21, 1821,

> *"I find myself often idle, vagrant, stupid, & hollow. This is somewhat appalling & if I do not discipline myself with diligent care I shall suffer severely from remorse & the sense of inferiority hereafter. . . . I need excitement."*

included a five hundred-person dinner paid for by wealthy students' parents. Parental contributions to the dinner resulted in their student having one of the twenty-one parts in the graduation ceremony. The larger the donation, the bigger the student's role. Emerson, who ranked number thirty in his class of fifty-nine, got to participate because some of the wealthy students turned down their parts.

As the class poet, a position he had gained after six others refused it, Emerson expected to deliver the original poem he had presented on Class Day in July. Instead he was assigned the role of John Knox in a dialogue among Knox, William Penn, and John Wesley, all famous religious thinkers of their day. Emerson had no interest in the views of any of these men and made no effort in the role. He had not memorized his lines well and had to be prompted frequently throughout the recitation. Emerson's lackluster academic performance did not qualify him for membership in the prestigious Phi Beta Kappa, causing him to remark as he left the campus: "A chamber alone, that was the best thing I found at college."

> *"A chamber alone, that was the best thing I found at college."*

As Emerson departed from Harvard, he became quite melancholy about his future. He knew he needed to earn some money before entering ministerial studies. Life at his mother's house was not conducive to rest and reflection about his future. His older brother William operated the School for Young Ladies in one room, and Robert Bulkeley, Emerson's mentally disabled younger brother, was there. Emerson discovered "a goading sense of emptiness & wasted capacity. . . . I am he

who nourished brilliant visions of future gran-
deur which may well appear presumptuous
and foolish now."

Unable to secure a teaching position
with the Boston Latin School because of
his poor rank in his graduating class, Emerson became the assistant in his brother William's school. Emerson did not like teaching.
His brother's strict soberness irritated him, and
the girls, only a few years younger than he,
easily embarrassed him, causing Emerson to
blush frequently. In later years, he recalled: "I
was nineteen; had grown up without sisters,
and, in my solitary and secluded way of living, had no acquaintance with girls. I still
recall my terrors at entering the school;
my timidities at French, the infirmities

of my cheek, and my occasional admiration of some of my
pupils . . . and the vexation of spirit when the will of the pupils
was a little too strong for the will of the teacher."

Chafing at the routine and the rules, he recalled going outside
to enjoy nature and gain "a moment's respite from this irksome
school to saunter in the fields of my own wayward thought . . .
when I came out from the hot, steaming, stove-ed, stinking, dirty,
a 'b'- spelling school room, I almost soared . . . at breathing the
free magnificent air, the noble breath of life."

Emerson received encouragement from his Aunt Mary to
spend more time with nature. So in the spring of 1822, William
and Emerson took a two-week walking tour. As they wandered
through the Connecticut Valley, slept outdoors, read books,
and did a little fishing, Emerson felt a complete escape from

the school. Although he enjoyed the different landscapes, he did not find the refreshment and stimulation of nature promised by Aunt Mary. When he told her, she responded that he should have gone alone.

Emerson returned for his second year of teaching, which went better than the first, and began to consider starting his studies for the ministry. However, William decided to go to Germany to study theology. He asked Ralph Waldo to take over his school; when he returned, it would be Emerson's turn to enter divinity school.

Ruth Emerson had recently moved to Roxbury, a woody rural stretch of farm country. It was within walking distance of Boston, meaning Emerson could continue teaching. His daily walks began to change his attitude about nature, and he wrote to a friend: "I am seeking to put myself on a footing of old acquaintance with Nature, as a poet should." This new setting, in which he confirmed how much he preferred the country to the classroom, eventually inspired his first poem that received any notice, "Goodbye, Proud World!"

GOOD-BYE, proud world! I'm going home:
Thou art not my friend, and I'm not thine.

O, when I am safe in my sylvan home

And when I am stretched beneath the pines,
where the evening star so holy shines,
I laugh at the lore and the pride of man,

For what are they all, in their high conceit,
When man in the bush with God may meet?

After William left for Germany, Emerson and his brother Edward continued the support of their mother, Robert Bulkeley, and their youngest brother Charles. Robert Bulkeley, who had never progressed mentally beyond childhood, went again to live with guardians in another town. Edward found a permanent teaching position in a boys' school, while at the same time studying law. Because Ruth Emerson had left Boston, Ralph Waldo rented a room for William's school in the back of a church. Although he managed to clear a profit, the future for the school was not promising. Most of the girls were getting too old for the school, and replacements were not enrolling.

Emerson decided the time had come for him to study for the ministry. He had been attending unofficially some of the lectures at Cambridge Divinity School, and he hoped to enter in the middle class to reduce the total years he needed to complete his studies. Emerson's personal religious beliefs had been evolving ever since his years at Harvard. William Ellery Channing, an instructor as well as the Unitarian minister at the Federal Street Church in Boston, had a tremendous influence on him at this time.

Channing believed that nature alone could not completely reveal God. Instead, God's word was the ultimate revelation of His nature. He further believed that man should rely on his own soul to determine truth and goodness because mankind's nature is like God's nature. Channing's belief in the individual's potential empowered Emerson, in later writings, to express his own ideas about the individual.

However, Channing's stance on the Christian belief in miracles brought the Unitarian minister in direct conflict with those who believed in the Trinity of God—the Christian doctrine that there is one God and three divine persons in the one God: the

Father, the Son (Jesus), and the Holy Spirit. Channing preached "Christianity is not only confirmed by miracles, but it is itself in its very essence, a miraculous religion." However, his Unitarian background allowed him to believe in only one God—not a three-in-one God. He therefore rejected what many Christians consider the greatest miracle, Christ's death and resurrection.

Channing left Harvard for a fourteen-month vacation in Europe. While he was gone, Emerson struggled with his own personal theology on such issues as God's nature, the necessity of evil, and the origin of man's moral sense. He came to believe that man gets his moral sense from the omnipotent mind of God, who acts upon and through man's finite mind. He completely rejected the Calvinistic views of his day regarding heaven and hell, although he believed in some kind of immortality, mostly in terms of the intellect. (Calvinism is a doctrine of the Protestant theologian John Calvin, who stressed that all events have been willed by God and that people are saved through God's grace and not by their own merits.) Emerson further believed that prayer was a means of communication between the finite mind of man and God's supreme Mind.

Emerson and William corresponded frequently, and Emerson read with interest his brother's changing ideas as he studied in Germany. William had met the German poet and philosopher Johann Wolfgang von Goethe, with whom he discussed the doubts raised by his German professors' teachings William was unable to free himself of the skepticism developed in his studies at the German university. Not knowing where his duty lay, he asked Goethe's advice about entering the ministry when he had so many doubts. Goethe suggested William not tell the world his questioning state of mind and go home to preach rather than disappoint his family, which counted on at least one new Emerson preacher each generation.

CHAPTER THREE

CALL TO MINISTRY

DURING THE LAST SIX MONTHS that William was in Europe, Ruth Emerson's family, the Haskinses, converted their old home in Boston into a thirty-five-room hotel, The La Fayette. Since his mother would receive about two hundred dollars a year from this venture, Emerson decided the time had come for him to apply to the Divinity School at Cambridge. On January 4, 1825, he wrote: "I have closed my school. I have begun a new year."

The next month, he received formal acceptance into the middle class and moved into Divinity Hall. Despite his desire to begin his training, he faced it with some apprehension. He believed that some of his character traits might work against him in a ministerial role—impatience with trite conversation, intolerance of human conceit, and a lack of ease around people that often resulted in his laughing at inappropriate moments. Emerson believed that he tended to criticize too severely and to praise too much. To make up for these defects, he vowed to maintain strict self-discipline and to act out the role of what he believed a minister should be. At this time, he did not consider that perhaps the ministry was not his best career choice. The preaching legacy of his ancestors weighed too heavily on him.

Almost immediately upon starting divinity school, Emerson began to suffer eye problems from all the reading. He could not take notes on the lectures and was excused from reciting in class because he could not keep up with the reading assignments. He also had to stop writing in his journals. Emerson developed other health problems—in his lungs, muscles, and joints—and withdrew from school temporarily. Having to leave his ministerial studies worried him, and the subsequent psychological stress adversely affected the physical problems he already had.

For a while, he went to an uncle's farm to see if rigorous work outdoors would help him regain his health. While Emerson worked in the fields, he talked to another laborer, a simple, uneducated man of the Methodist faith. The worker said that he believed that God granted all prayers, leading Emerson to remark that if so, people must be careful about what they asked for in prayer. This conversation would become the basis for the first sermon Emerson would preach in 1826.

With his health improving, Emerson began to tutor a few students, and in the fall of 1825 he assumed charge for a few months of a public school in Chelmsford, Massachusetts. He then moved to Roxbury for three months and finished his teaching in Cambridge in a house rented by his mother. There, he taught twenty boys for one semester. He also had to deal with

A nineteenth century engraving of farmers at work

issues involving his brothers. Edward, who had been diagnosed with tuberculosis, was keeping a rigorous schedule, teaching in Roxbury and studying law in Daniel Webster's office. With a sudden decline in his health, Edward went to the Mediterranean to recuperate in the warmer climate, leaving only Emerson to earn any income for the family.

Another problem was younger brother Robert Bulkeley. The people who had been serving as his guardians sent him home because he had become too difficult to manage. Ruth Emerson could not care for him, so Emerson took him to Chelmsford with him. However, Robert Bulkeley's condition worsened. He found a place in Chelmsford to board his brother, but Emerson had to provide the fees.

Then Emerson's older brother William returned from Germany and announced that he was quitting the ministry to study law in New York. Having almost died in a storm at sea on the return voyage, William decided that he could not accept Goethe's advice to pretend to his parishioners that he held beliefs that he really doubted. Because the youngest brother, Charles, still attended college, the family's entire financial burden fell on Emerson.

Emerson did not allow the family issues to overwhelm him, though. He took over Edward's school in Roxbury to provide support for his family, and he attended enough classes at the Divinity School to hold his place in the theological program. However, considering the family's dependence on him and his own unstable health, Emerson wondered if he should continue in the ministry. He wrote in his journal: "My years are passing away. Infirmities are already stealing on me that may be deadly enemies that are to dissolve me to dirt and little is yet done to establish my consideration among my contemporaries."

Even with his doubts, the Emerson history of having a preacher each generation once again burdened him. With William's switch to law and Edward's poor health, Emerson accepted that he was the only son who could fulfill this expectation. His mother rented a house near the college so Emerson could use one room to teach while still attending his classes at Cambridge. He kept the school open throughout the summer of 1826. One of his students was Richard Henry Dana Jr., who would later write the classic *Two Years Before the Mast.* When Dana's book was published, Emerson wrote to William: "Have you seen young Dana's book? Good as 'Robinson Crusoe,' and all true. He was my scholar once, but he never learned this of me, more's the pity."

In late summer, as the time for commencement neared, life seemed to settle for the Emerson brothers. William left for New York to study law; Edward headed home from the Mediterranean to continue working in Daniel Webster's law office; and Charles received first prize in the Boylston public speaking competition at Harvard. However, as Emerson started to study for his final exams, his health problems returned, and he experienced symptoms of tuberculosis.

Despite the setback, he appeared before the Middlesex Association of Ministries on October 10, 1826, and they gave approval for him to preach, even though his attendance had been irregular and he had not taken the usual examinations. He later said: "If they had examined me, they probably would not have let me preach at all."

Five days after his approval, Emerson preached his first sermon, "Pray Without Ceasing," in his Uncle Samuel Ripley's Waltham church. Emerson's mother, his Aunt Mary, and the congregation—many of them relatives who came to support him—packed the church. They received his words warmly. The following day as Emerson headed back to Cambridge, a farmer riding in the stagecoach with him told him: "Young man, you'll never preach a better sermon than that." The compliment especially pleased Emerson because the idea for the sermon had come from another farmer when Emerson worked on his uncle's farm.

Emerson preached his one and only sermon in congregations throughout the area. At that time, ministers preached all day—a lengthy sermon in the morning followed by an equally long one in the afternoon. The strain caused his health to deteriorate, with pains that he described as "the mouse in my chest." He also continued to suffer

"If they had examined me, they probably would not have let me preach at all."

eyesight problems. His doctors advised a long rest in a warmer climate. Uncle Samuel Ripley, who had financed Edward's trip to the Mediterranean for his health, now offered to pay for Emerson to go south. On November 25, a few weeks after Edward's return home, Emerson boarded the twenty-five sail *Clematis* for Charleston, South Carolina. When he could not tolerate the cold climate there, he moved on to St. Augustine, Florida.

He stayed in Florida through the winter months, spending most of his time alone walking the beaches or sailing. Emerson filled his journals with bits and pieces of sermon topics and with verse descriptions of St. Augustine and its people. He found the six-year-old town and its inhabitants rough and coarse. One practice that especially shocked Emerson was the slave auctions. He could not understand how the predominantly Spanish Catholics of St. Augustine could allow the terrible cruelty. As Emerson observed what he considered a societal failure, he more and more believed that each person's intuitive connection to God must be the individual's moral guide.

Fig. 4.

1, Course; 1a, Studding-sails; 2, Fore-topsail; 2a, Studding-sails; 3, Main-topsail; 3a, Studding-sails; 4, Mizen-topsail; 5, Fore-topgallant-sail; 5a, Studding-sails; 6, Main-topgallant-sail; 6a, Studding-sails; 7, Mizen-topgallant-sail; 8, Fore-royal-topsail; 8a, Studding-sails; 9, Main-royal-topsail; 9a, Studding-sails; 10, Mizen-royal-topsail; 11, Fore-skysail-topsail; 12, Main-skysail-topsail; 13, Mizen-skysail-topsail; 14, Fore-topmast-staysail jib; 15, Jib; 16, Flying jib; 17, Mizen spanker; 18, Spenser; 19, Main-royal-staysail; 20, Main-topgallant-staysail; 21, Mizen-royal-staysail.

A twenty-five sail ship similar to the one Emerson took on his voyage to Charleston

The fragmentary sermon ideas recorded in his journals continued to reveal the theological questions that nagged him. Emerson spent days trying to understand the meaning of the atonement, a doctrine that describes how someone can be forgiven by God. But one question only led to another, until he began to doubt first the omnipotence of God and then even the existence of God. He was determined not to let others know of his doubts, and he planned to practice the conventional faith just in case it were true, and until he assured himself that they were real doubts, not just passing questions. His brother William had rejected Goethe's advice to practice the same duplicity that Emerson now planned.

After he had gained some weight and experienced an overall improvement in his health, Emerson began the journey home in March 1827 on the sloop *William*. There he met a fellow passenger, Achilles Murat, nephew of Napoleon Bonaparte and a professed atheist. Their trip should have taken only two days, but a storm blew the ship off course, stretching the voyage to ten days. Emerson and his cabin mate Murat spent almost the entire time in conversation, and a quick friendship developed. The two should have had little to discuss, but Emerson found himself admiring the Frenchman for a number of reasons, one of which was Murat's robust health. Little did Emerson know that Murat would die at age forty-six while Emerson would survive him by thirty-five years.

During their time together on the ship, Emerson enjoyed Murat's bold skepticism, his frankness, his sincerity, his great knowledge, and his passion for the truth. Murat returned the admiration, even going to some Unitarian churches to hear Emerson preach his new second sermon, "The Uses of Unhappiness," each time the ship docked. Their meeting caused Emerson to believe that his faith had been tested and survived. It also caused him to wonder about the relationship of morality to a belief in God. Murat appeared to be a moral person, even though he denied God's existence. This paradox caused Emerson to have his first tolerance for nonbelievers.

On his way home, Emerson stopped in New York to visit William. While he was there, Edward notified him that First Church in Boston wanted Emerson to preach for several weeks while their pastor, Reverend Nathaniel Frothingham, went on a European vacation. With the cold weather gone, Emerson looked forward to preaching in his father's former church. He preached multiple sermons there, earning ten dollars for each, and enjoyed time with his family at the Manse in Concord. However, after the numerous preaching requests he started to receive after Reverend Frothingham returned to First Church, he found the crowded rooms not conducive to writing more sermons. He refused three separate offers to assume the full pastorate of a church. Still not feeling physically strong enough to take on such responsibility, he told William that "I am all clay, no iron."

By this time, he had increased the number of sermons from which he could select, but he continued his practice of reading them to the various congregations. For now, the churches loved him because he repeated the familiar beliefs that had always comforted them. This amicable period would not last, as Emerson began to examine and question every doctrine. He would begin to speak only what he truly believed, even if those beliefs contradicted Unitarian church doctrine.

During the Christmas season, Emerson accepted an invitation to go to New Concord, New Hampshire, to preach for three Sundays. He soon regretted his decision because of the sixty-mile journey. To add to his regret, he received a more desirable offer to preach in another town. Already committed to New Concord, he prepared to be cold and bored in the small village of about 3,500 people. The Unitarians in New Concord planned to build a new church under the leadership of a prominent citizen, Colonel William Kent. He had a large family composed of children from his first marriage and of children belonging to Margaret Tucker, a wealthy widow who had become his second wife. One of his sons, Edward Kent, had been Emerson's classmate at Harvard. Three of the children still lived at home, including Margaret Tucker Kent's daughter, sixteen-year-old Ellen.

Ellen had tuberculosis, and although the disease was in the early stages, cold weather prevented her from hearing Emerson preach the Christmas sermons. When they first met in her home, Emerson scarcely talked to her. He had never had any young female friends. Although he recently had written in his journal that he longed for a friend who would listen to all he wanted to say, at that time he was referring to a male friend. However, he found himself frequently recalling Ellen's quiet nature.

After completing the three sermons, Emerson returned to the Divinity School, where he continued to write in his journals. His health still concerned him, and he told his brother William: "I am living cautiously yea treading on eggs to strengthen my constitution. It is a long battle this of mine betwixt life & death & tis wholly uncertain to whom the game belongs."

Emerson also continued to face problems with his brothers. Edward, in his weakened condition because of the lung disease, had overtaxed himself while studying to become a lawyer. Suddenly, Edward went into uncontrollable rages marked by fainting and delirium. The fits required two men with him at all times to control his outbursts. Emerson had to commit Edward to the McLean Asylum, where his brother Robert Bulkeley was also a patient.

By the end of the year, Edward had regained mental stability, but he would never be physically strong enough to continue his studies or to practice law. He exiled himself to Puerto Rico in the West Indies, where he worked as a clerk. He died unexpectedly in 1834, and Emerson began to wonder how many members of the family would be affected by mental illness. He felt little fear for himself, however, as seen in a journal entry: "I have little apprehension of my own liability to the same evil. I have so much mixture of silliness in my intellectual frame that I think Providence has tempered me against this."

Emerson met Ellen Tucker again, and this time he talked to her and began to consider romance. Ellen, with her heart-shaped face, curly black hair worn in a pompadour, and tiny waist, had entertained several other suitors, but no one compared to Emerson. Their courtship progressed rapidly, and Emerson proposed marriage to Ellen on December 17, 1828. She was seventeen years old, eight years younger than Emerson.

Ellen suffered more and more from the tuberculosis, often spitting blood. The recommended treatment was to take long carriage rides over bumpy roads to loosen the phlegm in her

Emerson and his new wife would have ridden in a carriage much like this one.

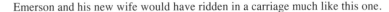

chest. Emerson faithfully followed the recommendation, taking Ellen for frequent jarring rides. Early in January, Ellen and her family visited Boston so that Emerson and Ellen could spend more time together and so that Ellen could receive treatment from Boston doctors. The trip in wet weather caused Ellen's lungs to hemorrhage.

About the same time, the Second Church in Boston invited Emerson to serve their church while their ill pastor, Henry Ware Jr., took a leave for his health. The position would at first be as an assistant, but upon his return, Ware planned to accept a professorship at Harvard Divinity School.

Although gratified by the invitation, Emerson first needed to be sure that Ellen could safely live in Boston, or whether she needed to live in a warmer climate. He told his younger brother Charles: "She is too lovely to live long." However, he believed that even for a short time "it would still have been a rich blessing to have been permitted to have loved her."

Dr. James Jackson, a leading Boston physician, examined Ellen and assured Emerson that her tuberculosis was still in an early, curable stage. She could safely live in Boston. Emerson decided to accept the Second Church's offer to become their junior pastor at a salary of $1,200 per year, and he was ordained on March 11, 1829. He developed a friendly relationship with his new parishioners. Some of them were intellectuals seeking mental stimulation.

Emerson preached the traditional Unitarian doctrine, but he no longer emphasized historical teaching. He replaced it with his own belief that the order found in nature and the divine voice present in each person's heart took the place of such study.

Becoming the minister of an important church was not always easy for Emerson. His hardest duty was the many visits he had to make as a pastor—five a day on average. He struggled with having to write a sermon each week, had trouble praying aloud because he always felt he had to use the proper word, and for the most part did not enjoy hymns because of his lack of musical ability. Believing that many of the old hymns presented a false theology, he printed a new hymnal for his congregation's use.

Upon hearing about Emerson's acceptance as pastor of the Second Church, Mary Emerson immediately delivered her opinion about what was happening in Emerson's life. She believed that he needed to know poverty for a longer time before accepting such a prestigious assignment. She feared that marrying a young woman who had money of her own would further separate him from God. However, her opinion failed to sway her nephew, so she turned her efforts to writing letters instructing Ellen about what she must do to become a suitable wife for a man destined for greatness.

In early September, Emerson and Ellen took a trip to the White Mountains as part of her tuberculosis treatment. She had already been riding horseback every day to increase her strength. For their trip, the couple rode in a horse-drawn carriage with two

wheels while Ellen's mother followed in a covered carriage in which Ellen could ride if it rained. The couple had a wonderful time, giggling and creating silly rhymes, as they covered almost two hundred miles on the ten-day trip. The outing was successful in loosening phlegm in Ellen's chest, and she felt strong enough to marry.

After the trip, Emerson returned to Boston for a few days to make housing arrangements for Ellen's family, who planned to move there for a while after the wedding. Then, on September 30, he returned to Concord to take Ellen Louisa Tucker as his bride. Reverend Moses Thomas performed the ceremony in the Kent home. Charles, Emerson's youngest brother, was the only person in Emerson's family to attend the wedding.

The couple enjoyed a brief honeymoon, from which Ellen showed no ill effects. Emerson, however, had sprained his knee just before the wedding. It still bothered him enough when he returned to his church that he walked with a cane and could not stand to deliver his sermons, instead having to read them while sitting on a chair. Aunt Mary did not meet Ellen until the following March, when she wrote to her nephew Edward, "I like her better than I dreamt."

As a newlywed, Emerson led a life that was basically without problems. He wrote to Aunt Mary: "There's an apprehension of reverse always arising from success. . . . I cannot find in the world . . . any bulwark against this fear." However, when Reverend Ware returned from his trip and resigned, he was pleased with the way Emerson had fit into the church. Ware told the congregation: "Providence presented you at once a man on whom your hearts could rest."

All the duties associated with the Second Church pastorate transferred to Emerson, who carried out his responsibilities in a careful and able manner. Emerson also became interested in Boston's civic affairs. He was elected to the school board and served as chaplain of the state Senate. Although not directly involved in political issues, he did invite anti-slavery speakers to the church. In his personal studies, he became more and more interested in literature, especially that of such contemporaries as Thomas Carlyle, Samuel Taylor Coleridge, William Wordsworth, and Goethe. At the same time, he found his enthusiasm for the pastoral role diminishing.

Emerson worried most, though, about the health of his young wife. She had begun to decline almost immediately after their marriage and, in early January 1831, suffered another bleeding attack. She temporarily rallied and continued the carriage rides that they believed would heal her lungs. In February, after going out to ride in snow so deep that Emerson canceled Sunday morning worship, Ellen became ill. This time, nothing could prolong her life. As she lay near death, Ellen's main concern was for the family she was leaving behind, especially for her husband of only seventeen months. On her final day, a Sunday, Emerson did not preach but sat at her bedside as she relapsed and then died at nine o'clock that evening, February 8, 1831. She was only nineteen years old.

Charles, who had kept the bedside vigil with his older brother, later wrote to Aunt Mary: "She spoke this afternoon very sweetly of her readiness to die. . . . She saw no reason why her friends should be distressed—it was better she should go first, & prepare the way—She asked Waldo, if he had strength, to read her a few verses of scripture—and he read a portion of the XIV chapter of John—Waldo is bowed down under the affliction, yet he says 'tis like seeing an angel go to Heaven."

Emerson himself wrote to his Aunt Mary only two hours after Ellen's passing. The letter reflected his conflicting emotions regarding his young wife's death—grief over his loss but gladness that her suffering had ended: "My angel is gone to heaven this morning & I am alone in the world & strangely happy. Her lungs shall no more be torn nor her head scalded by her blood nor her whole life suffer from the warfare between the force & delivery of her soul & the weakness of her frame." Reverend Ware preached the funeral sermon, and at Ellen's request, she was buried in her father's tomb at Roxbury.

Over the next several months, Emerson's journals, letters, sermons, and poems—everything he wrote or said—reflected his grief. In June, Harvard invited him to deliver the Phi Beta Kappa address, but he declined because he was still mourning. Every day he visited Ellen's tomb, walking from Boston to Roxbury. One time he even opened Ellen's coffin, an action he would repeat in later years at the grave of a young son.

"My angel is gone to heaven this morning & I am alone in the world & strangely happy."

CHAPTER FOUR

COPING WITH ADVERSITIES

FTER ELLEN'S DEATH, Emerson wrote more than one hundred sermons, some of which expressed traditional theology and some of which barely stayed within the limits of liberal Christianity. However, most of the congregation received his sermons with gratitude. One regular parishioner said: "In looking back on his preaching I find he has impressed truths to which I always assented, in such a manner as to make them appear new, like a clearer revelation. He is truly an angel to me, a real messenger from heaven."

However, about eighteen months later, Emerson resigned as minister of Second Church over the Christian sacrament of Communion. Communion, also known as the Eucharist, commemorates the death of Jesus. Worshippers share bread and wine (the elements of Communion), in a reenactment of the Last Supper, where the words of Jesus are spoken—"This is my body" and "This is my blood."

Emerson did not believe that Jesus Christ intended the Last Supper to be reenacted over and over through Communion. He believed that the traditional observance, in fact, repudiated all that Jesus taught about releasing men from formal rituals and laws. He believed that true communion was spiritual, between an individual and God.

When Mary Emerson learned that her nephew had resigned from the church, she wrote him a critical letter. The stress of the broken ties to his church and to Aunt Mary, the lingering mourning over Ellen's death, and the diarrhea that had plagued him for months left Emerson weak both physically and emotionally. He abruptly decided to go to Europe to recuperate. After writing a farewell letter to his former congregation, Emerson sailed from Boston on Christmas Day, 1832, on the brig *Jasper*.

He landed in Malta on February 2. Despite having eaten nothing but pork and beans throughout the weeks-long voyage, he felt healthier and stronger. He traveled throughout Italy, visiting churches and other attractions, and arrived in London in July, where he enjoyed a visit with British poet and critic Samuel Taylor Coleridge.

He then endured a rough sea voyage to Glasgow, where he hired a carriage to take him to the secluded home of Scottish essayist and historian Thomas Carlyle. Carlyle invited Emerson to stay overnight, and over the next twenty-four hours, the two developed a friendship that lasted the rest of their lives.

Next, Emerson visited the great British poet William Wordsworth at Wordsworth's rural Rydal Mount home. Wearing green goggles for his inflamed eyes, the sixty-three-year-old Wordsworth greeted Emerson and took him for a walk around the gardens, where Wordsworth composed much of his poetry. The white-haired poet chatted in an easy, friendly manner, expressing definite opinions, especially regarding America. Emerson had read and admired Wordsworth's poetry since his junior year in college, and was honored to meet him.

Wordsworth and Carlye did not meet Emerson's expectations, though, because neither showed any religious insight. In a letter a few days after his visit with Wordsworth, Emerson wrote that he "had met with men of far less power who had got greater insight into religious truth."

Restored to health, Emerson was ready to go home. He left England in September 1833 and arrived in New York a month later. He then traveled to Boston. On the journey home Emerson wrote in his journals ideas about self-reliance, which he later developed into essays. "A man contains all that is needful to his government within himself," he wrote. "He is made a law unto himself. All real good or evil that can befall him must be from himself. He only can do him-

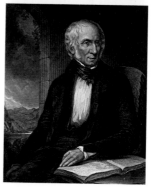

From top to bottom: British poet Samuel Taylor Coleridge, Scottish essayist and historian Thomas Carlyle, and British poet William Wordsworth.

William Wordsworth's rural Rydal Mount home in the Lake District of England

self any good or any harm. Nothing can be given to him or taken from him, but always there's a compensation. . . . The purpose of life seems to be to acquaint man with himself. . . . The highest revelation is that God is in every man."

After his return, Emerson continued to accept preaching invitations but began to appear as a public lecturer, as well. In August, he delivered his first lecture, "The Uses of Natural History," in Boston. These earliest lectures, which have never been published, mainly concerned his nine-month trip to Europe, where he had expanded his knowledge of history and science. Through his travels, he met the manufacturer of the world's best microscopes in Florence, Italy, saw a natural history exhibit in Paris, and in Liverpool talked to the man who invented the English locomotive. His lecture topics began to reflect these new interests, and even after he moved on to new subjects, he contin-

"The purpose of life seems to be to acquaint man with himself. . . . The highest revelation is that God is in every man."

ued to think about scientific discoveries. From science he went to biography. He began to present lectures on a group of men that he would later include in a book.

During that same time period, Emerson began to search for a place in the country where his brothers and he could live. Emerson had the money to provide this country place because the estate of his deceased wife Ellen finally had been settled. Emerson received the first half of Ellen's share of the Tucker estate, which totaled more than $11,000. Moreover, income from those assets provided about $1,200 a year, almost two-thirds of his former pastoral salary. But before Emerson could complete plans for all the brothers to live together, Edward died unexpectedly in Puerto Rico of tuberculosis on October 1, 1834, at the age of twenty-nine.

About eighteen months after his return from Europe, Emerson became engaged to Lydia Jackson, whose roots stretched back to Colonial times. Lydia had first met Emerson when she attended a Boston church where he was preaching. They met several more times, and Emerson finally wrote her a letter proposing marriage.

The relationship between Emerson and Lydia was much different from the one Emerson had with his first wife, Ellen. Although Emerson admired Lydia, he did not feel for her the passion that he had for Ellen. The day after the announcement of his and Lydia's engagement, Emerson wrote to William: "I announce this fact in a very different feeling from that which I entered my first connexion. This is a very sober joy." Several weeks later, Emerson was still writing about Ellen in his journal. There was no mention of Lydia.

Except for his aunt, Mary Emerson, all of Emerson's family liked Lydia, who had a quick wit and keen intelligence. After a brief courtship, the couple married on September 14, 1835. Lydia always called him "Mr. Emerson," and he changed her name to "Lidian" because it sounded more melodious with Emerson.

After the ceremony in Lydia's family home in Plymouth, Massachusetts, Emerson took his new bride to a large house on two acres that he had purchased for $3,500 the previous July. Emerson spent the rest of his life in the plain, square wooden house on the outskirts of Concord. The spacious grounds in the rear sloped to a meadow divided by a brook. To the south lay Walden Pond.

A few months after her son's marriage, Ruth Emerson moved in with Emerson and Lydia. She would remain there for eighteen years until her death at age eighty-five. Emerson had finally realized his earlier dream of providing a permanent, comfortable home for his mother.

Before Emerson had time to settle into his rural retreat with its vegetable gardens and numerous fruit trees, the citizens of Concord in 1836 elected him hog-reeve, a position reserved for the most recently married man. His job was to round up stray hogs and turn them over to a pound keeper, who fed them until their owner paid a fine and reclaimed them. Emerson had to perform this function until another man married. He also served on the school committee and became one of three standing members for the Concord Social Library.

While working with the community, Emerson also dealt with personal problems. He had become completely estranged from Aunt Mary, who despised his new religious views so much that she vowed never to enter his home again. Of more concern to Emerson was the poor health of his youngest brother, Charles. The two were not only brothers but best friends. A year earlier, Charles had started working in the law offices of his fiancée's father. Charles and Elizabeth Hoar were waiting to get married in September, by which time Emerson would have finished adding rooms to his house for them.

In early April, after suffering from a severe cold for more than a month, Charles was diagnosed with advanced tuberculosis. Their older brother William offered to care for Charles if Emerson brought him to New York. After getting Charles settled with William and seeing that Charles appeared to be improving, Emerson returned to Salem, where he was delivering a series of lectures.

On May 7, Emerson received a letter from William saying that Charles's health was rapidly failing. Emerson left for New York. But on May 9, before he completed the trip, Charles died. Emerson wrote in his journal, "Now commences a new and gloomy epoch in my life; I have used his [Charles's] society so fondly and solidly . . . . I have felt in him the inestimable advantage . . . of finding a brother and friend in one."

Until Charles's remains could be returned to Concord, they were supposed to be kept in a friend's tomb. Before the casket was placed there, someone removed the nameplate on it and destroyed the identification. Charles's body was never sent to Concord. Despite his mourning, Emerson continued to receive visitors to his home. During this time, he began a relationship that would be one of the most important of his life. In July, Margaret Fuller arrived as Lidian's guest in what stretched into a three-week visit.

Margaret Fuller had been educat-
ed in a way usually reserved for sons.
She was a noted conversationalist,
and at Harvard, she had become an
intellectual friend of Emerson's classmate Frederic Hedge. With a strong,
forceful personality, she once told
Emerson: "I now know all the people
worth knowing in America, and I find
no intellect comparable to my own."
Emerson did not dispute her claim.

When Margaret was in her early
twenties, she had walked out of a
church service one day, dissatisfied

Margaret Fuller (1810–1850)
was a journalist, critic and
women's rights activist.
She was the first full-time
female book reviewer in
journalism.

with what she was hearing. She aimlessly walked around the
grounds, finally settling by a stream. As she sat there meditating,
a shaft of sunlight illuminated both her body and her spirit, and
she realized for the first time that she was connected to a higher
being than herself. This moment of self-revelation corresponded
to the ideas that Emerson was developing for a book on nature,
and they had deep conversations about their ideas.

After she departed, Emerson described her in his journal as
"a very accomplished & very intelligent person." Over the next
ten years, they would remain in close contact with each other.

Emerson continued to lecture around the Boston and Concord areas. He spoke to increasingly larger and larger audiences
He was not as successful in his attempts to write poetry. However, once while walking in the woods, he saw a flower bloom-
ing in an out-of-the-way place. As he pondered the flower's purpose, he composed "The Rhodora," which contains some of his
most famous lines:

Rhodora! if the sages ask thee why
This charm is wasted on the earth and sky,
Tell them, dear, that if eyes were made
    for seeing,
Then Beauty is its own excuse for being:
Why thou wert there, O rival of the rose!
I never thought to ask, I never knew;
But, in my simple ignorance, suppose
The self-same Power that brought
    me there brought you.

On September 8, 1836, Emerson met with a small group of writers, ministers, and free thinkers at a Cambridge hotel to plan a symposium for people who, like themselves, considered the state of modern American thought "very unsatisfactory." The group wanted to explore "deeper and broader views," and came to be known as the Transcendental Club, though Emerson referred to it by several different names, including the Aesthetic Club.

Eleven days later the group met a second time and from then on its membership expanded rapidly. Most club meetings focused on a single topic, such as "American Genuis," "Education of Humanity," "Is Mysticism an Element of Christianity?" and "Does the Species Advance Beyond the Individual?" At a meeting at Emerson's home, the topic was on "the Inspiration of the Prophet and Bard, the nature of Poetry, and the causes of sterility of poetic inspiration in our Age and Country."

The formation of the Transcendental Club was, in many respects, a protest against the rigid, traditional teachings of Harvard and Cambridge. At the time, Harvard had

Top: Bronson Alcott, founder ot the Temple School. Bottom: Henry David Thoreau, writer

a president, eleven professors, and seven instructors, while an average meeting of the club drew almost a dozen "members."

Anyone who attended meetings was a member, but all shared a common dissatisfaction with the state of philosophy, religion, and literature in America. They included New England's intellectual elite: Emerson's Harvard classmate Hedge; Fuller, a champion of women's rights; abolitionist James Clarke; Orestes Brownson, a former Unitarian minister and future founder of the Workingman's Party in New York; Boston minister George Ripley, who founded and led the Brook Farm experiment in communal living; Bronson Alcott, founder of the controversial Temple School, which accepted both boys and girls and, most unusually, one black student; American Indian rights activist Elizabeth Peabody; and Henry David Thoreau, a writer and lifelong abolitionist who preached civil disobedience in order to bring about a just government.

Emerson had received his introduction to transcendental beliefs in 1833 when he read an article in the *Christian Examiner*. It was written by Hedge. Before becoming a minister, Hedge had studied in Germany. At the time of this article's publication, Hedge served at a Unitarian church in Bangor, Maine. His article was the first published in America on the ideas of German philosopher Immanuel Kant, who believed that while no one can understand God, the soul, or the world in the way we understand things in nature, individuals must believe in God, in immortality, and in free will.

The American Transcendentalists believed that intuition was just as reliable a source of truth and knowledge as was scientific investigation. They believed that God continuously displayed his presence everywhere in the natural world and to all persons, regardless of occupation, economic status, or gender. The Transcendentalists lacked trust in all inherited religious forms and rituals. Instead they urged a return to nature, and reliance on an inner conscience that transcends ordinary logic.

CHAPTER FIVE:

THE PRIVATE INDIVIDUAL

IN SEPTEMBER 1836, Emerson anonymously published *Nature,* a slim, ninety-five page book, bound in brown cloth. In it, he expressed how much nature in all its forms had come to mean to him.

He conceived an ideal universe in which all its interrelated parts, including the natural world and the human mind, mirrored each other. In such a universe, he explained how "a leaf, a drop, a crystal, a moment of time is related to the whole, and partakes of the perfection of the whole. Each particle is a microcosm, and faithfully renders the likeness of the world."

Throughout the book, Emerson shared his experiences with nature, and he urged the men of his generation to establish an original, primary relationship with nature rather than settle for

a secondhand one described in past writings. "Why should w
grope among the dry bones of the past?" he wrote. "The su
shines today also."

A writer in the *Democratic Review* praised the book for i
evidence of "the highest imaginative power" while "it prove
to us that the only true and perfect mind is the poetic." Despi
such approval, it took twelve years for the initial five hundre
copies to sell. Those twelve years, though, became the most cr
ative period of Emerson's life.

On October 30, 1836, Emerson and Lidian's first child,
boy they named Waldo, was born. Emerson wrote in his journ
the following day: "Last night at 11 o'clock, a son was born
me. Blessed child! a lovely wonder to me, and which makes tl
Universe look friendly to me."

Despite Emerson's opposition to rituals, he recorded in h
journal that when Waldo was christened, he was dressed "in tl
self-same robe in which, twenty-seven years ago, my broth
Charles was baptized."

In December at the Masonic Hall in Boston, Emerson bega
a series of ten lectures on "Human Culture." The series showe
how each part of the individual provides man the keys to
larger, more general aspect of life. To attract large audience
Emerson advertised the lectures and left tickets for sale at
central location.

The lectures especially impressed a young attorney, Horac
Mann, who in the next decade would so revolutionize nineteen
century educational practices that today he is known as tl

This statue in Lexington, Massachusetts, is commonly called *The Lexingt*
Minuteman. Sculpted by Henry Hudson Kitson and erected in 1900, it depic
Captain John Parker. The statue is located where the Revolutionary War start
in 1775.

"father of education." Mann wrote in a letter that Emerson "from his central position in the spiritual world, discovers harmony and order where others can discover only confusion and irregularity. His lecture last evening was one of the most splendid manifestations of a truth-seeking and truth-compelling mind I ever heard."

On July 4, 1837, Concord belatedly celebrated the sixtieth anniversary of the Battle of Lexington. Back in 1776, the day after Paul Revere had warned Americans that British troops were coming, the colonists' militia, the Minutemen, took their stand on the bridge that led to Concord. There, they defended themselves in the first battle of the American Revolution. For the dedication of the new monument honoring these brave men, Emerson wrote "The Concord Hymn." The first verse, later carved on the Minuteman statue, has become famous:

> By the rude bridge that arched the flood,
> Their flag to April's breeze unfurled,
> Here once the embattled farmers stood,
> And fired the shot heard round the world.

In August, Emerson delivered the Phi Beta Kappa address to the Harvard graduating class. Emerson began by calling for an end to America's dependence on other nations for its literary thought: "Our day of dependence, our long apprenticeship to the learning of other lands, draws to a close."

Emerson stated that mankind had become so divided through performing narrow, minute tasks that the whole man had been lost. Society had become "one in which the members have suffered amputation from the trunk, and strut about so many walking monsters,—a good finger, a neck, a stomach, an elbow, but never a man. . . . In this distribution of functions the scholar is the designated intellect. In the right state he is Man Thinking."

Emerson contended that institutions have further hampered Man Thinking: "The book, the college, the school of art, the institution of any kind, stop with some past utterance of genius. . . . They pin me down. They look backward and not forward." This statement angered many of those in the audience who were part of the institutions Emerson denounced.

He continued by stating that the first and most important influence on Man Thinking is nature. He further warned that too much time spent with books creates a bookworm, not a Man Thinking, and reminded his listeners that "meek young men grow up in libraries, believing it their duty to accept the views which Cicero, which Locke, which Bacon, have given; forgetful that Cicero, Locke, and Bacon were only young men in libraries when they wrote these books." Finally, Emerson told his audience that "the world is nothing, the man is all; in yourself is the law of all nature."

Although Emerson's remarks offended about half his audience, others felt enlightened. James Russell Lowell, an eighteen-year-old student who would become a famous poet, critic, and satirist, said that Emerson's address was considered "an event without any former parallel in our literary annals, a scene to be always treasured in the memory for its picturesqueness and its inspiration."

Oliver Wendell Holmes Sr., one of the most highly regarded poets of the nineteenth century, called the "American Scholar" address, or oration, "our intellectual Declaration of Independence." Friends urged Emerson to publish the speech. He would, and within a month of its printing, the first five hundred copies sold out.

Oliver Wendell Holmes Sr. was an American essayist, humorist, and poet. He was also a physician and professor of anatomy and physiology at Harvard, and is recognized as a medical reformer.

After the speech, Emerson and Lidian returned to Concord, where the next day the Transcendental Club met. By now its membership had grown to fourteen and included Henry David Thoreau. Like Emerson, Thoreau was a journal writer, and the two discussed possibilities for a Transcendental journal in which the writings of Thoreau and others could be published. One by one, Emerson gained the respect of this Concord circle, eventually becoming the unofficial leader of the Transcendentalists.

In July 1838, the six young men in the graduating class of the Divinity School at Cambridge asked Emerson to deliver their commencement speech. In the speech, Emerson called for direct, individual religious experiences instead of stale, inherited ones, telling the audience that man can be free only after he disconnects from the past. Emerson challenged the prospective preachers: "Wherever a man comes, there comes revolution. The old is for slaves . . . cast behind you all conformity, and acquaint men at first hand with Deity." He believed that man could reach God directly without benefit of a mediator between himself and God.

Then Emerson shocked the Protestant community by claiming that Jesus was an ideal model for all humans, but not God. Emerson believed that Jesus perfectly understood the spiritual and moral laws, and that his authority arose from his perfect grasp of those transcendental laws. "Alone in all history, he estimated the greatness of man. One man was true to what is in you and me," Emerson told his audience.

Although some called Emerson a heretic and an infidel, Orestes Brownson gave him the benefit of the doubt in his October 1, 1838, article in the *Boston Quarterly Review*: "His real object is not the inculcation of any new theory on man, nature or God; but to induce men to think for themselves on all subjects, and to speak from their own full hearts and earnest convictions."

Most of Emerson's family—with the exception of Aunt Mary, who believed the address was inspired by the devil—supported Emerson throughout the controversy. Such backing became somewhat awkward for Emerson's uncle, Samuel Ripley, who had always let his nephew preach in his church whenever Emerson visited him. After the uproar over the Divinity School Address, Emerson told his uncle that he did not want to speak from the pulpit.

This presented a dilemma for Ripley. If Emerson did not preach, the congregation would erroneously conclude that Ripley had banned him. Ripley told Emerson either to come prepared to preach or to stay home. The battle waged on in print and in pulpits for many months until the antagonism finally died down. But Emerson did not receive another invitation to speak

Harvard for the next forty years. From that point on, he would spend his time as lecturer and author.

On February 24, 1839, Lidian, after a difficult pregnancy, gave birth to their second child, a daughter, whom she named after Emerson's first wife. Emerson wrote in his journal: "Lidian, who magnanimously makes my gods her gods, calls the babe Ellen. I can hardly ask for more for thee my babe, than that name implies. Be that vision & remain with us, & after us."

If Lidian hoped to remove the ghost of the first Ellen, she failed. Lidian even read Ellen's letters aloud to Emerson, who apparently did not think it strange that his present wife was reading his deceased wife's letters. Over the years, he never seemed to notice how hard Lidian tried to reach his heart.

In September, members of the Transcendental Club again discussed the possibility of starting their own journal. Although all of the members believed a journal was a good idea, no one wanted to assume responsibility for it. Finally, Margaret Fuller agreed to become the editor.

The first issue of the quarterly magazine appeared on July 1, 1840. A subscription cost three dollars per year, and at first

The *Dial* was an American magazine that started in 1840 and served as the chief publication of the Transcendentalists. Emerson said, "I wish we might make a Journal so broad & great in its survey that it should lead the opinion of this generation on every great interest & read the law on property, government, education, as well as on art, letters, & religion."

they had approximately 250 subscribers. Fuller and Emerson solicited articles from various sources for the *Dial,* a name proposed by Bronson Alcott. The magazine became a venue for Fuller's advocacy of women's rights and also provided some of the first American translations of Buddhist and Hindu scriptures.

However, the number of subscribers steadily declined. Even those who supported transcendental views found the magazine too otherworldly, and Emerson himself wished they had more articles on politics and economics.

Those who had never heard Emerson speak thought his writings were unorganized and unfocused. Those who had heard his lectures found the same themes they had heard previously. The main difference between the lectures and the writings was that the essays were more polished and had more examples. Many of these same essays appeared in Emerson's first collection, *Essays, First Series,* published in March 1841. In it, Emerson would express the essentials of his Transcendentalist faith.

CHAPTER SIX

FLUX OF LIFE

One theme to which Emerson returned again and again in *Essays, First Series* was that of self-reliance. With compact sentences and no connecting words or phrases, Emerson hammered out an essay that called for the individual to become self-reliant. "Trust thyself: every heart vibrates to that iron string. . . . Nothing is at last sacred but the integrity of your own mind."

He observed, however, that there are obstacles to self-reliance. One of these is trying to please others: "What I must do is all that concerns me, not what the people think." He further warned that others will not approve of the man who goes his own way: "For non-conformity the world whips you with its displeasure."

Emerson added that the other danger to self-trust is worrying about consistency—about whether today's actions and words are the same as those of the past. However, he believed such concerns are not the mark of a great soul, which must change as its intuition perceives new truths: "A foolish consistency is the hobgoblin of little minds, adored by little statesmen and philosophers and divines. With consistency a great soul has simply nothing to do."

Emerson contended that the self-reliant person should not worry if others accuse him of contradicting himself. All of the great minds of the past were misunderstood: "to be great is to be misunderstood." Emerson concluded that to understand the concept of self-reliance, one must put it in the proper context of "God-reliance."

Emerson faced controversy regarding his premise—that while the spiritual and natural worlds share the same laws, they are also distinct. Man, he believed, connected the two. A popular idea that he ridiculed was that wicked people enjoy all the fruits of this life, while the good have to wait for reward in the afterlife. Such a fallacy, he declared, precluded any justice in this life.

Emerson's book received mixed reviews. One critic praised it, saying the book contained "many single thoughts of dazzling brilliancy; much exquisite writing, and a copious vein of poetical illustration." On the other hand, Emerson's Aunt Mary regretted that he "had

'Trust thyself: every heart vibrates to that
ron string. . . . Nothing is at last sacred but
he integrity of your own mind. "

ot gone to the tomb amidst his early honors" instead of writing
uch a disgraceful work. Emerson made only a small profit on
ne book, leaving him with financial problems. To raise money,
e prepared a series of eight lectures in 1841 that he called "On
ne Town." He planned to present them in Boston as an explana-
ion of transcendentalism. However, the average income for his
ectures dropped by seventeen dollars in Boston, so he had to
xpand his circuit to include New York.

Horace Greeley, a former New England farmer who founded
he *New York Daily Tribune,* was making money by crusading
or new ideas. While in New York, Emerson had several conver-
ations with Greeley about transcendentalism. Greeley's push
vas for greater industrialization, a concept with which Emerson
ould not agree because it was in direct opposition to his call for
elf-reliance. Although the two clashed philosophically, Greeley
ublished full reports on all of Emerson's six lectures at the Li-
rary Society.

Another young editor, Walter Whitman, reported the lectures
nd thirteen years later, Walt Whitman would publish his first
ook of poetry, *Leaves of Grass,* whose title was taken from a
emark made by Emerson in one of these addresses. The New
York lectures brought in the money Emerson needed to pay his
ills, and he headed home.

Back in Concord, Emerson found himself at odds with his
wn group of Transcendentalists who wanted to establish an

Walt Whitman (1819 – 1892) was a poet, essayist, journalist, and publisher. Regarded as one of the most influential and innovative poets of America, he is often called the father of free verse. His work was very controversial in its time, particularly his poetry collection *Leaves of Grass,* which was considered immoral and indecent because of its overt sexuality.

ideal community. Out of this desir grew their idea for Brook Farm both an educational establishmen and a place where people coul work with their hands to avoid in dustrialization. Each member chos his own type of labor and his work ing hours. The association guaran teed rent, fuel, food, and clothing t each member. Emerson opposed th communal idea and refused to par ticipate in the Brook Farm experi ment, which averaged about sevent members.

However, Emerson did want t see changes in society, so he decide to try experiments on his own. Th first of these was to invite Bronso Alcott and his family to live in th Emerson home for a year. Since th closing of the Temple School, Alcott had little income and hi family lived in near-poverty. If they lived with the Emersons, th Alcotts had to agree to practice plain living and exchange thei labor for board and room. The Alcotts declined the proposal Emerson then moved to his second idea of inviting the maid an the cook to eat with the family at the dinner table. The maid wa willing to try; the cook refused, causing the maid to change he mind.

Not having succeeded with his first two plans, Emerso turned to a third—arranging for young Henry David Thoreau t spend a year with the Emersons. Thoreau's position as a teach er had ended with the school term, and he had no employment except occasionally helping his father manufacture pencils. In extending the invitation to Thoreau, Emerson told the younger man he could work at whatever jobs he chose in exchange for room and board. The skilled Thoreau accepted, and he worked hard during the day either in the house or in the garden. In the evening, he rowed Emerson on the Concord River, where the two discussed their transcendental views. Thoreau's visit lasted well past the original year.

During the summer of 1842, the Emersons met their new neighbors, Nathaniel Hawthorne and his wife, Sophie. Thoreau helped them settle and planted a vegetable garden for them; he also taught Hawthorne how to row a boat and how to fish. The two soon became good friends. Although Emerson tried to be friendly to Hawthorne, the men found conversation difficult and never developed a close relationship.

On November 2, 1841, Lidian gave birth to their second daughter. Emerson had gone to Boston on business and did not arrive home in time for the birth. Upon learning that he had a new daughter, Emerson suggested naming her Lidian. His wife refused, and the couple quarreled. Lidian prevailed, and they named the child Edith.

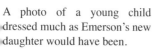

A photo of a young child dressed much as Emerson's new daughter would have been.

A nineteenth century engraving of a Sunday afternoon outing

Because Emerson had grown up without a father, he enjoyed being a good father to his children. Although he loved all of them, he adored Waldo, who it seemed could do no wrong in his father's eyes. Yet Waldo was a normal, mischievous child who had a hot temper. Waldo had little patience with Ellen, who was three years younger. The two fought with each other as siblings do. She stepped on his sand castle; he pushed her away. When Ellen knocked over his tower of blocks, Waldo knocked her down.

Largely because of the adoration of his father and other relatives, young Waldo thought the world revolved around him. One time Thoreau made Waldo a wooden whistle. Just as Waldo blew on it, he heard the rumble of thunder. He told Thoreau: "My music makes the thunder dance."

On January 27, 1842, at the age of five, Waldo suddenly died, of scarlet fever. Both Emerson and Lidian mourned the tragedy deeply. Every place Emerson looked—his study, the sandbox, the barn—reminded him of time spent there with Waldo. In April, Emerson began to write an elegy he called "Threnody," or funeral song. Into the work he poured his deep grief, but the pain became so great that he could not finish the poem at that time. Emerson had lost all belief in an afterlife, so he did not believe he would ever again see his beloved son. He wrote:

The South-wind brings
Life, sunshine, and desire.
And on every mount and meadow
Breathes aromatic fire;
But over the dead he has not power,
The lost, the lost, he cannot restore;
And, looking over the hills, I mourn
The darling who shall not return.

Lidian suffered as well. Whenever she left the house, she wore a long black dress and a long black veil. The garden became Lidian's refuge; she dreaded company and could not, even a year later, shake off her melancholy. Emerson wrote in his journal the deep sorrow that Lidian had confided to him: "I wish I had never been born. I do not see how God can compensate me for the sorrow of existence."

Little three-year-old Ellen grieved as well. She could not understand where he had gone, and she kept moving from window to window to look outside to see if he were hiding behind a tree. One time she asked her grandmother why God could not stay by himself with the angels and let Waldo come down to play with her. At mealtimes she always asked if God was feeding Waldo.

In the spring, Emerson resumed some of his regular responsibilities. He also took over editorship of the *Dial* because Margaret Fuller was too ill to continue. In August, she asked Emerson if she could come for a month's visit so that he could help her finish an article she was writing for the *Dial*. The Emersons already had Thoreau living with them as well as another house guest. Lidian was trying to take care of baby Edith while still mourning the loss of Waldo. Nevertheless, Emerson gave Fuller permission to come, and she stayed for forty days.

Emerson and Margaret took long walks together, causing Lidian to question their relationship. Lidian first confronted Margaret, and then at dinner that night made a scene that Emerson ignored. As Lidian's suspicions of an illicit relationship grew, she became sadder and sadder, with her mood matching her somber mourning clothes.

From time to time, Emerson hinted in his journals that since Waldo's death, he and Lidian lived as brother and sister rather than as man and wife. Because he allowed Margaret to read his journals, these comments increased Margaret's hope that she and Emerson might develop the romantic relationship that she wanted. When the Emersons' second son, Edward Waldo, was born the following year, Margaret realized that Emerson's hints about having a brotherly relationship with Lidian

Emerson's second wife Lidian and their second son Edward Waldo

were untrue. Margaret came for no more long visits. Despite the additional worry that Emerson caused Lidian, he had little patience with her continued gloom over Waldo's death. Emerson told his brother William: "It is high time for her to get a good deal better."

By March 1843, the number of *Dial* subscribers had dropped to 220, and sales of the magazine were not covering expenses. While Emerson paid to cover the shortage, he tried to make the periodical more pertinent to the times.

Bronson Alcott had returned from England, a trip for which Emerson had raised funds and contributed from his own pocket. Emerson had tried to connect his two friends, Alcott and Thomas Carlyle, by writing to Carlyle: "You may love him [Alcott], or hate him, or apathetically pass by him, as your genius shall dictate: Only I entreat this, that you do not let him go quite out of your reach until you are sure you have seen him & know for certain the nature of the man."

However, no matter how hard they tried, the two men were not compatible. Alcott found Carlyle's conversation trivial, cynical, and humorless. Carlyle perceived Alcott as a simple-hearted, impractical dreamer. Nevertheless, for the sake of their friendships with Emerson, the two attempted a relationship. Carlyle invited Alcott back for dinner on a second visit. When Alcott refused the meat dishes because of his vegetarian preferences, Carlyle tried to provide a special treat the next morning at breakfast by serving choice strawberries. When Alcott dumped the strawberries in his mashed potatoes and stirred them together, Carlyle became nauseated and left the table. The two quarreled on their third and final visit.

When Carlyle learned that Alcott had returned to America accompanied by some British visionaries, he wrote to Emerson

Fruitlands was an idealized agrarian commune, based on Transcendentalist principles, established in Harvard, Massachusetts, and co-founded by Bronson Alcott. Residents of Fruitlands ate no animal substances, drank only water, bathed in unheated water, and did not use artificial light. Additionally, property was held communally, and no animal labor was used. The community lasted only seven months and was not considered a success.

and warned him to be careful of any plans they might propose. One of the men and Alcott bought a farm for another experiment in communal living, which they called Fruitlands. Alcott moved his family to the farm in June and tried to put into practice his many impractical theories. By the following January, Fruitlands had failed. Emerson helped purchase a home for the Alcotts, where Bronson proved he could be an expert gardener and landscaper. However, he was never able to support himself and his family.

Throughout the time of the Fruitlands experiment, Emerson busily lectured from Maine to Maryland. In January, he expanded his itinerary to an even larger geographical area because he needed the money. The increased territory also brought a new series of lectures on New England—its spiritual history, manners, customs, trade, and religion. In 1844, Emerson's lectures began to reflect the rising excitement in America over westward expansion. In June, Emerson bought stock in the controversial local railroad scheduled to run between Concord and Boston. He also continued to support the Concord library that he had helped found two years earlier.

Emerson did not lecture during the winter months, devoting himself instead to a new volume of nine essays that represented

Spirit of the Frontier by John Gast, 1872. Manifest Destiny was the nineteenth-century belief that the United States was destined by God to expand across the North American continent, from the Atlantic seaboard to the Pacific Ocean. The term was used in 1845 by a New York journalist to call for the annexation of Texas. It was used by Democrats in the 1840s to justify the war with Mexico. The belief in an American "mission" to promote and defend democracy throughout the world, as expounded by Abraham Lincoln, Woodrow Wilson, and Ronald Reagan continues to have an influence on American political ideology.

his experiences. The essay "Experience" added the idea of flux to his theories about nature. Since the flow of life is inevitable, Emerson urged man to move with it. "Life is a train of moods like a string of beads, and, as we pass through them they prove to be many-colored lenses which paint the world their own hue, and each shows only what lies in its focus." The volume of essays received the usual mixture of praise and criticism.

About this same time, Emerson became involved in the slavery issue. He had shown an interest in the problems of slavery since his time as a preacher, when he allowed anti-slavery speakers in his church, and since he observed slave auctions in Florida. However, until this time he had never taken an active role. Emerson felt compelled to move from his position as an observer and become involved in the politics of the issue. To

A 1937 photograph of a little girl on the Alabama plantation of her slave ancestors

the citizens of Concord, he gave a speech that celebrated the "Emancipation of the British West Indies." This address, which was a clear, effective expression of the moral issues involved, was Emerson's first public statement on slavery.

While Emerson entered the political arena, Thoreau was building a one-room hut by Walden Pond on land owned by Emerson. This was the culmination of an idea Thoreau had considered for a long time. He wanted to live alone in a house he built himself, and planned to raise his own food and buy only a few essentials that he could not grow.

In this isolation, he would be independent, free of any responsibilities, and able to decide what he wanted to do with his life. Thoreau was actually only a couple of miles from the heart of Concord, and since he had helped his father build a home near the center of town for the family, the citizens of Concord could not figure out what he was doing. Thoreau stayed in his cabin on Walden Pond for about two years and wrote his first book, *A Week on the Concord and Merrimac Rivers.*

The Emersons decided to try their own change in living arrangements. For some time Lidian had been ill, and Emerson had hired Sophie Ford to serve as the children's teacher and governess. However, they did not relinquish all control over the children, and they expected Ford to observe a strict regimen. First, the children had to follow a vegetarian diet. Ellen later recalled that she had never tasted meat until she was at least eighteen years old. She also remembered that "we were to have a pail of cold water splashed over us every morning. We were to be made active and hardy, trained to write a diary and taught sewing as well as lessons."

In an effort to further reduce Lidian's responsibilities, the Emersons decided to hire a housekeeper and live as boarders in their own home. After they hired Marston Goodwin, the Emersons kept only four rooms for themselves. They allowed Goodwin to bring her own four children to live there and to take in other boarders as well. Emerson had enjoyed a large household ever since his younger days when his mother took in boarders. With Goodwin managing all the household chores, the Emersons had more time together as a family. They especially enjoyed outdoor activities, such as picnics and picking huckleberries. Goodwin remained with the family for about sixteen months.

For several years, Emerson had worked to get his poems together for publication. Several friends who had circulated some of his poems persuaded him that they were worthy of publication. However, when he was unable to find a publisher that pleased him, Emerson returned to the lecture circuit. In December 1845, he gave a series of seven lectures, all biographies, called "The Uses of Great Men" at the Boston Lyceum. This became his most successful series, both financially and in popularity, as he presented it more than thirty times over the next two years.

Six of the lectures featured what Emerson called great, or representative, men—Plato, Swedenborg, Montaigne, Shakespeare, Napoleon, and Goethe. Emerson would publish these seven lectures in 1850 as *Representative Men.*

Toward the end of the next year, Emerson finally found a publisher for his poems, James Munroe & Company of Boston, and the first edition of 1,500 copies was published on December 26, 1846. The book, containing fifty-nine poems, began with one of his most difficult, "The Sphinx." Easier poems such as "The Rhodora," were scattered among the others. "Concord Hymn" concluded the book. As with his essay collections, Emerson's book of poetry received mixed reviews.

The *Boston Courier* called it "one of the most peculiar and original volumes of poetry ever published in the United States."

However, Orestes Brownson, who had recently converted to Catholicism, called the poems "hymns to the devil." James Russell Lowell, who in the next year would publish *A Fable of Critics,* believed that even the worst poems were "mines of rich matter." Emerson took pride in the volume he called his "little white book" because it was bound in white cloth. He sent gift copies to more than 150 of his friends and relatives.

About the same time that Emerson found a publisher for his poems, he renewed his interest in fruit trees that had begun with the planting of fifteen apple trees ten years earlier. When his brother William sent Emerson a box of grapevines, he planted them in the two-acre field east of his house. With new enthusiasm, he began keeping records of the varieties of trees, and he soon had more than one hundred fruit trees of various kinds—plum, peach, apple, pear, and quince. The names alone must have appealed to the poet in him— Golden Drop, Early Rose, Bellflower, and Bloodgood.

CHAPTER SEVEN

TAKING A STAND

Tending fruit trees was not enough to relieve Emerson's restlessness, and he decided to accept an invitation to lecture in England. He hoped to also visit France, and he hired a tutor to give him lessons in conversational French. Emerson departed from Boston aboard the *Washington Irving* on October 5, 1847, and reached Liverpool two and a half weeks later.

Upon his arrival, he found awaiting him a letter from Thomas Carlyle. The note contained an enthusiastic invitation for Emerson to visit Carlyle and his family. Since Emerson had a week before his lecture schedule began, he eagerly accepted the invitation to visit the friend he had not seen for fourteen years, although the two had corresponded. When the men met, they had so much to share that they could not quit talking.

Emerson wrote long letters to Lidian in which he showed a deep affection for his children. He told her that sometimes he was tempted to run away from his obligations to come home and see them. However, he did not say that he missed Lidian and ignored reports of her own loneliness and illness.

Next, Emerson traveled to France, where he lectured for twenty-five days before returning to London. There, he gave one more series of six lectures, at the Portman Square Literary and Scientific Institution.

When Emerson arrived in America on July 27, he had been gone nine months. He returned home in high spirits and good health. He enjoyed time with his children, composing lullabies to sing to them at bedtime, and joined in their outdoor activities. He visited with his mother, who still lived in his home, and went to New York to see William.

After the publication of *Representative Men* in January 1850, Emerson widened the area of his lecture tours to include the West. These western trips, on which Emerson often endured harsh traveling conditions, would eventually span a period of twenty years as he repeatedly took his message to the American frontier. Emerson worked hard for six to eight hours a day preparing his lectures, but he no longer had to deal with *Dial* magazine. His trip to Europe had been the final blow to the struggling transcendental magazine's publication.

That same summer, Emerson received the sad news of Margaret Fuller's death. Margaret had gone to Europe a year before Emerson made his second trip there. She settled in Italy, where she met and secretly married the Italian revolutionary Giovanni Angelo Ossoli, a marquis who had been disinherited by his family. The next year, they had a son but still did not reveal their marriage. Instead, they sent the boy away to be cared for by a peasant woman who nursed him.

Margaret and Ossoli became involved in Italy's attempt to free itself from Austrian domination, and had to flee during the siege of Rome. Eventually, they were able to make plans to sail to America. She left Italy on May 17 with her husband and her son to sail to New York. During the trip, the captain died of smallpox and the boat was quarantined. Finally, on July 15 they approached the American shore just ahead of a hurricane. Only sixty miles from the coast, the ship wrecked on Fire Island and sank, taking with it all passengers aboard. Emerson lamented her death for many days, writing eight entries in his journal regarding the loss of a special friend.

As Emerson was increasing the scope of his lecture tours as far west as the Mississippi River, controversy over slavery spread throughout the nation. The annexation of Texas into the United States after the end of the Mexican War intensified the battle over slavery. There were strong disagreements as to whether or not slavery should be extended into new territories. U.S. senators Stephen Douglas and Henry Clay proposed a compromise bill designed to preserve the union.

The Fugitive Slave Act was included in the compromise. It became the most controversial part of the entire document because it required citizens to help in catching runaway slaves. Former slaves who had already settled in the North panicked and fled to Canada. Daniel Webster, under whom Emerson's brother Edward had studied law, spoke

"An immoral law makes it a man's duty to break it, at every hazard."

Stephen Arnold Douglas (1813 – 1861) was a politician from the state of Illinois. Nicknamed "The Little Giant" for his short stature, large head, and broad shoulders, Douglas was known as a great orator. In 1854 he introduced the highly controversial Kansas-Nebraska Act that allowed people of the new territories to decide for themselves whether or not to have slavery.

in Congress in favor of the terms of the compromise. Emerson could not believe that the great orator whom he had so admired and who had been a guest in his home could be, in his estimation, such a traitor. In scathing words, Emerson said: "The fairest American fame ends in this filthy law."

Emerson's intense resentment surprised even his closest friends. Now, in regard to the Fugitive Slave Law, Emerson declared: "I will not obey it, by God." He began to speak out from his lecture platforms, urging others not to obey it as well: "An immoral law makes it a man's duty to break it, at every hazard."

Emerson's increasing involvement in public issues brought a subtle change to his voice and style. While the essays of his younger days dealt with timeless issues, his words now reflected interest in the problems of his contemporary society. Slavery and other social issues led him to a new understanding of the importance of ethical principles and action as part of one's spirituality. Ethical action became for Emerson not just an outgrowth of religious belief but religion's very essence. For Emerson, the spiritual life came to be less of a private matter and more of a striving to help others in a selfless way.

Two years after Margaret Fuller's death, several publishers asked Emerson to write her memoir. At first, Emerson declined because he did not think she had been an important enough literary figure to warrant such recognition. However, when the publishers persisted, Emerson began to collect her letters and other papers and discovered that she had been more popular than he had realized. Emerson agreed to write the memoir with the help of two other editors. The two-volume memoir was released in Boston in 1852.

That same year brought the publication of Nathaniel Hawthorne's *The Blithedale Romance,* a novel loosely based on the Brook Farm experiment. In the story, the main female character, Zenobia, is pictured as an immoral woman because she is so self-reliant. Most people considered Margaret Fuller to be the thinly disguised model for Zenobia.

While Emerson worked on Margaret's memoirs, he also wrote new lectures and continued work on his book about England. All of the reading and writing caused his eyes to bother him again, and he bought his first pair of glasses. In June, his mother's health diminished after she rolled out of bed during a nightmare and broke her hip. Although her doctor predicted that she would never walk again, Emerson refused to believe him.

His mother did regain some mobility, enough to go on buggy rides, but never enjoyed good health again. On her eighty-fifth birthday, Ruth Haskins Emerson died, while Emerson was lecturing in Charleston, South Carolina. Crushed that he was not there, Emerson wrote to William: "After living with her so long, I feel as if I might have been present at the moment of her departure."

Four years later, Emerson moved the bodies of his mother and his son Waldo to a new burial plot that he had bought in Concord's Sleepy Hollow cemetery. Just as he had once looked into the coffin of his dead wife Ellen, he now looked into Waldo's coffin. At the time, Waldo had been dead for fifteen years.

In 1856, after years of planning, Emerson published *English Traits,* based upon his two trips to England. Both Americans and the British received the book well, with one critic saying that there was "no better book by an American about Victorian England." Within a month, the book sold 3,000 copies and went into its second printing of 2,000 copies. Emerson left the book sales to others, however, as he headed back to the lecture circuit. He interrupted his travels in the spring to recover from the measles.

By 1858 Emerson, at age fifty-five, was beginning to tire of the lecture circuit. He was away from home for weeks and months at a time, and he had to endure train travel, poor hotels, inadequate lecture halls, and exposure to many kinds of weather conditions. All of them affected his physical well-being. Adding to his problems was the situation with Aunt Mary, who had changed her mind about never entering Emerson's house again. She did not live in her nephew's home but was close enough to upset the household with her irritating personality. Finally, Emerson got her to agree to go to Williamsburg, Long Island, where she remained the rest of her life with a niece. The following spring, Robert Bulkeley, Emerson's mentally ill brother, passed away.

In October 1859, abolitionist John Brown, for whom Emerson had arranged speaking engagements in the Concord Town Hall, intensified the North-South conflict when he attacked the military arsenal at Harpers Ferry in order to arm slaves to help free themselves. While he held sixty citizens hostage, Brown expected their slaves to come join him. None did. Soldiers under the leadership of Colonel Robert E. Lee easily quelled the rebellion. The survivors were quickly tried, sentenced, and executed for treason. John Brown was hanged on December 2, 1859. Emerson, who had earlier supported Brown's stance against slavery, wrote to his brother William that Brown was "a true hero, but lost his head there." Emerson gave public eulogies in Concord and in Salem, Massachusetts, on the day of Brown's execution.

The year 1860 brought the publication of *Conduct of Life,* Emerson's third collection of essays. All had been drawn from lectures originally delivered in Pittsburgh, Pennsylvania, in 1851. Because the book confirmed moral principles based on eternal laws, its release a few months before the outbreak of the Civil War seemed to fit the sentiments of that time. However, the book did not actually mention the impending crisis. Clearer in style and easier to read than some of Emerson's previous works, the book appealed to a wider audience. Some of the essays, including "Wealth"

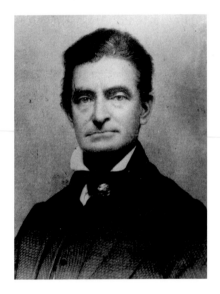

John Brown (1800–1859) was a dedicated abolitionist who led twenty-one men on a raid of the federal arsenal at Harper's Ferry, Virginia (now West Virginia) in 1859. Within thirty-six hours of the attack, however, most of Brown's men had been killed or captured. Many historians agree that Brown's attempt to start a slave revolt escalated the tensions that led to secession and the American Civil War.

and "Power," offered practical advice. Others, such as "Beauty," defined at length a particular trait: "Things are pretty, graceful, rich, elegant, handsome, but, until they speak to the imagination, not yet beautiful."

Typical for Emerson, the book received mixed reactions. His longtime friend Thomas Carlyle called it Emerson's best book: "You have grown older, more pungent, piercing,—I never read from you before such lightning-gleams of meaning as are to be found here." On the other hand, Thoreau wrote in his journal about the book: ". . . wants the fire and force of the earlier books."

Emerson paid little attention to reviews because in April his son Edward developed typhoid fever, an illness that lasted for many weeks. Although Edward's sisters, Ellen and Edith, provided good nursing care, he remained in poor health for several years. Ellen, who was now twenty-one years old, began to act as her father's secretary and treasurer. This new responsibility followed years of her and Edith's management of the household because of their mother's many illnesses.

The November 1860 election of Abraham Lincoln to the presidency was welcome news to Emerson, who hailed it as "sublime, the pronunciation of the masses of America against Slavery." Emerson, like many others, believed that Lincoln would immediately free the slaves. However, Lincoln had another priority: preserve the Union. Confederate artillery shots fired on Fort Sumter on April 13, 1861, brought cries for war.

Despite his support for the war, Emerson balked at his son Edward's desire to enlist. Only seventeen years old, Edward had

Abraham Lincoln, in a top hat, with Allan Pinkerton and Major General John Alexander McClernand at Antietam. Lincoln took a great interest in the details of the war. Preserving the Union initially took priority over freeing the slaves.

never regained his strength after battling typhoid fever. So in stead of heading to war, he entered Harvard. But he soon returne home, weak from trying to keep up with his college courses an embarrassed that he could not be among the many classmate who had left school to join the war effort.

Like other families, the Emersons were affected financiall by the war. Book sales, lecture income, and stock dividends wer all down. Lidian could not rent a piece of property she owne in Plymouth, and Emerson could not find a buyer for a woodlo The fees for lectures in and around his home dropped to an aver age of twenty-five dollars. So when the Smithsonian Associatio in Washington offered him to come lecture for a fee of $84, h quickly accepted.

Emerson hoped, while in Washington, to speak to some hig officials, even the President if possible, about issuing an eman cipation proclamation. Emerson and others of similar beliefs di not like Lincoln's delay in handling the slavery issue and did nc agree with his apparent emphasis on preserving the Union.

On January 31, 1862, Emerson delivered his lecture "Ameri can Civilization," in which he denounced slavery, a system tha allowed men to eat "the fruit of other men's labor." He remaine in Washington for three days after the address and met briefl with President Lincoln, who impressed Emerson more favorabl than expected.

The war continued, with wooden ships *Monitor* an *Merrimack* fighting to a draw on March 9. A month later, 23,00 men died at the Battle of Shiloh. On May 6, Henry David Thc reau died of tuberculosis at the age of forty-four. Thoreau ha known for some time that he was dying and talked openly abou his impending death. Emerson composed his last major piece c writing, "Thoreau," to honor his friend. Emerson also gave the funeral address.

Shortly after Thoreau's death, Emerson's son Edward got the chance to go west, as he had long desired. He left in May, but by the time he arrived in San Francisco after a long trip by rail and stagecoach, he concluded that he needed to serve in the war effort rather than fulfill his own goals. He decided to return home immediately and boarded a ship. He didn't reach New York until October, when he learned that the previous month Lincoln had issued a preliminary Emancipation Proclamation. Emerson himself read about Lincoln's proclamation in a monthly magazine. He received the message with joy and gratitude. Edward's return to Concord further gladdened his heart.

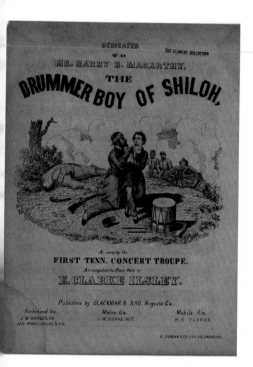

The Battle of Shiloh, immortalized here in song, was one of the bloodiest conflicts of the American Civil War. The Battle, also known as the Battle of Pittsburg Landing, was fought on April 6 and 7, 1862, on the Tennessee River in southwestern Tennessee. Confederate forces launched a surprise attack against the Union Army but were forced to retreat. Nearly 24,000 men died as a result of the fighting, and of those, 13,047 were Union soldiers. No one imagine there would be bloodier battles to come in three more years of war.

CHAPTER EIGHT

SPIRIT UNBOUND

On January 1, 1863, when the Emancipation Proclamation took effect, Boston held a great celebration. Emerson agreed to write a poem for the occasion if his name did not appear beside it. He feared that he might not be able to get the verses just right. The poem that opened the program that day, "Boston Hymn," contained twenty-two four-line verses that celebrated the slaves' freedom. One verse read:

> To-day unbind the captive,
> So only are ye unbound;
> Lift up a people from the dust,
> Trump of their rescue, sound!

These lines brought those in the audience, many of whom were former slaves, to their feet.

The next several years Emerson faced the death of family members and friends. On May 1, 1863, Emerson's aunt, Mary, died at the age of eighty-nine. He wrote to his brother William: "Her genius was the purest . . . her letters & journals charm me still as thirty years ago, & honor the American air." A year after Aunt Mary's death, Emerson's fellow author and neighbor, Nathaniel Hawthorne, died at the age of fifty-nine.

Despite the deaths, Emerson continued his own demanding lecture schedule, presenting seventy-seven lectures in 1865 alone. The assassination of Abraham Lincoln by John Wilkes Booth touched Emerson deeply, and a few days later Emerson presented a moving elegy, telling his audience: "We meet under the gloom of a calamity which darkens down over the minds of good men in all civil society, as the fearful tidings travel over sea, over land, from country to country, like the shadow of an uncalculated eclipse over the planet." He concluded his final tribute to Lincoln with these words: "Rarely was a man so fitted to the event."

Despite his hectic schedule, Emerson found time for family matters, as well. In October, his youngest daughter Edith, at age twenty-three, married William H. Forbes, a young lieutenant colonel who had been a prisoner of war. William and Edith had enjoyed a close friendship for a number of years. Emerson approved of his daughter's choice and wrote to a friend: "This event has brought great joy to this house, for he is a noble youth."

In April 1867 *May-Day and Other Poems* was published—Emerson's second book of poetry, published twenty years after his first volume. The new book contained "In Memoriam," the seven-page poem about Emerson's brother Edward, who had died thirty-three years earlier. Another poem, "Terminus," revealed Emerson's awareness and acceptance of his own aging:

It is time to be old,
To take in sail:—
The god of bounds,
Who sets to seas a shore,
Came to me in his fatal rounds,
And said: "No more! . . . "

Although Emerson claimed that his body was failing, he gave eighty lectures in 1867, and his beliefs remained as strong as ever. In July, Harvard appointed Emerson to its board of overseers, and the Phi Beta Kappa chapter invited him to deliver its commencement speech. Thirty years earlier, Emerson had delivered his famous "The American Scholar" to the Phi Beta Kappans. This time his topic was "The Progress of Culture," which ranged from women's right to vote to cultural minorities.

The delivery did not go well. Emerson had never used glasses to read his lectures but now discovered that he could not see the words. However, he was not ready to give up the lecture schedule and started on a western tour in the fall. This time, though, Ellen traveled with him.

The year 1868 brought another death—Emerson's older brother William. William's death at the age of sixty-five left Emerson as the only surviving sibling. Although William had been ill for several years, his death was unexpected. On the day William died, Emerson went to New York on business and stopped by William's house, where the

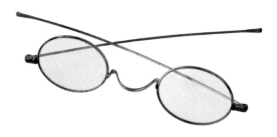

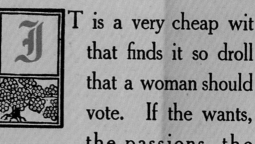

T is a very cheap wit that finds it so droll that a woman should vote. If the wants, the passions, the vices, are allowed a full vote, through the hands of a half-brutal, intemperate population, I think it but fair that the virtues, the aspirations, should be allowed a full voice as an offset, through the purest of people.

—*Ralph Waldo Emerson.*

A flyer from the time, with a quote from Ralph Waldo Emerson, supporting the right of women to vote.

two brothers visited for half an hour. Emerson was grateful to have seen his brother on the day of William's death.

Two years later, Emerson published *Society and Solitude,* an accumulation of essays from his earlier days. And, that same year Harvard invited Emerson to participate in a new graduate school program by delivering eighteen lectures. Although his memory was failing, Emerson accepted but soon found he had difficulty fitting lectures to a schedule.

As Emerson's energy started declining, Lidian became quite active. She finally accepted her daughter Ellen's role as manager of the house and as Emerson's secretary and started a social life of her own. Her new happiness allowed her to encourage her husband to accept an invitation from John Forbes, their son-in-law's father, to join his family on a trip to California. With his wife, children, and doctor all urging him to go, Emerson accepted.

Emerson had traveled extensively by train for his many lecture tours, but never before in a Pullman railroad car. He enjoyed all the luxuries the trip provided. After arriving in San Francisco, Emerson gave several lectures that were eagerly attended by Californians. However, after the first few, Emerson suspended the lectures until he could visit the state's natural resources. He became enchanted with the orange trees, grapes, flowers, sea lions, mountains, and sequoias. In the Yosemite Valley, Emerson met John Muir, a thirty-three-year-old naturalist, who begged Emerson to stay longer in order to explore more of the natural wilderness.

In the summer of 1872, the crackling sound of fire awoke Emerson early one morning. After determining that the sound was fire and not rain, Emerson tried to douse the flames with water. However, the fire was inside the walls, and smoke filled

he attic. Emerson and Lidian were home alone, and after calling Lidian to waken her, Emerson rushed outside in a pouring rain and shouted to his neighbors for help. Then he ran back inside to retrieve a couple of manuscripts. His neighbors responded immediately, carrying out furniture, clothing, and household items before the slate roof caved in. Somehow Emerson's study, with all his books and papers, escaped the fire. That night, Emerson wrote in his journal: "House/burned, 24 July [1872]."

Emerson set up his study in the Concord courthouse, which was not being used at the time. He, Lidian, and Ellen went to live at the Old Manse while they made plans to rebuild. Although the Emersons had $2,500 in insurance, enough to cover the costs, gifts totaling $12,000 came from friends and neighbors to pay for the restoration and for a vacation while the repairs took place.

The whole ordeal exhausted Emerson. When his health suddenly worsened, his son-in-law wrote to the publishers to postpone for a year the contractual due date for *Letters and Social Aims*. With that pressure temporarily removed, family urged him to go abroad to recover his health, but he could not decide what he wanted to do. He told his family: "When nature indicates that it is time, it is more graceful to retire at once, not to seek the world."

Fearing that death might be near, Emerson tried to decide what should be done with his unfinished manuscripts after he was gone. These decisions further stressed Emerson. He reached a point where he had trouble recalling words and names. Meanwhile, the "Emerson fund" continued to grow, and he finally agreed to make the trip. On October 23, 1872, Emerson and his daughter Ellen sailed for England on the steamship *Wyoming*.

Yosemite National Park, California

Edward met his father and Ellen in Liverpool, and the next day they traveled to London. Emerson met many of his old friends, including Thomas Carlyle. Emerson wrote to Lidian about the visit: "Yesterday I . . . spent two or three hours with Carlyle in his study. He opened his arms and embraced me . . . we sat down and had a steady outpouring for two hour and more."

On May 15, Emerson and Ellen sailed from Liverpool on the *Olympus*. They arrived in Boston the day after Emerson's seventieth birthday. His daughter Edith and her husband William Forbes met them at the dock because Concord residents had asked Edith to delay her father's arrival in Concord until the afternoon, when they had a great homecoming celebration planned.

Emerson agreed to spend some time in Boston. As the train approached Concord, the engineer began to blow the whistle When the train stopped, Emerson was amazed to see a huge crowd at the station. He was even more astonished to learn that the people were there to celebrate both his birthday and his return home. As a band played "Home, Sweet Home," Emerson embraced his wife, Lidian.

The celebration continued with a parade of carriages down Main Street and out to the Emerson property entrance, which was decorated with a huge arch of flowers and leaves. Emerson and Lidian got out of their carriage and walked between rows of singing children to the front door of their restored home. Emerson thanked his cheering neighbors for "this trick of sympathy to catch an old gentleman returned from his wanderings."

Although Emerson's physical condition had improved, his memory had not. Despite the memory problems, Emerson managed to pull together *Parnassus*, an anthology of his favorite poems written by other authors. The book brought in $1,000 profit only nine months after its publication. In the same year, Emerson's son Edward finished his medical training abroad, came home, and married.

In September of 1879, the Unitarian church in Concord invited Emerson to its fiftieth anniversary observance. Emerson's only contribution to the ceremony was a faltering reading of a hymn. By now, Emerson had stopped writing in his journals and had stopped writing letters as well. He told a friend: "I have reached an age when I no longer remember what I have written."

On February 10, 1881, Emerson appeared before an audience for the last time. He spoke to the Massachusetts Historical Society about Thomas Carlyle, who had recently died. As Emerson praised his old friend that day in Boston, the funeral for Carlyle was being held in Ecclefechan, Scotland.

"I have reached an age when I no longer remember what I have written."

A year later, Emerson suffered from a cold after being caught in a rainstorm, and died on April 27, with Lidian by his side. The Unitarian church bell tolled seventy-eight times. In four weeks, Emerson would have celebrated his seventy-ninth birthday.

The next day, the family held a private service. The black walnut casket was then moved to the

Unitarian church, where a thousand people attended the funeral services. Bronson Alcott, whom Emerson had supported both financially and emotionally for almost fifty years, read a sonnet he had written to Emerson.

Emerson was buried in the family plot in Sleepy Hollow near the graves of his former neighbors, Henry David Thoreau and Nathaniel Hawthorne. A pine tree stood at the head of Emerson's grave. Later a large granite boulder, selected by Emerson before his death, was placed in front of the tree. On it were carved some of Emerson's own words:

The passive Master lent his hand
To the vast soul that o'er him planned.

Emerson's grave, Sleepy Hollow, Massachusetts

TIMELINE

1803   Born in Boston, Massachusetts, on May 25.

1806   Begins education in Dame School at age three.

1811   Father, William Emerson, dies on May 12.

1812-17 Attends Boston Latin School.

1817-21 Attends Harvard College; graduates on
August 21, 1821.

1820   Begins keeping journal; continues rest of life.

1821-25 Teaches school.

1825   Admitted to middle class of Harvard Divinity School.

1826   Approved by Middlesex Association of Ministries
to preach; preaches first sermon; goes to Florida
to improve health.

1827   Meets Ellen Louise Tucker in Concord,
New Hampshire.

1828   Commits brother Edward Emerson to McLean
Asylum; becomes engaged to Ellen Tucker on
December 17.

1829   Ordained into ministry at Second Church, Boston;
marries Ellen Tucker on September 30.

Sculpture of Ralph Waldo Emerson by artist Frank Duveneck at the Cincinnati Art
Museum, Cincinnati, Ohio

1831   Ellen dies on February 8.

1832   Preaches sermon on Communion; resigns from Second Church; leaves on trip to Europe on Christmas Day.

1833   Meets Samuel Taylor Coleridge, William Wordsworth, and Thomas Carlyle; develops interest in science; gives first public lecture in Boston.

1834   Brother Edward Emerson dies unexpectedly in Puerto Rico on October 1; moves to Concord, Massachusetts, where he stays rest of life.

1835   Buys house in Concord; marries Lydia Jackson; meets Bronson Alcott.

1836   Brother Charles Emerson dies suddenly; publishes first book, *Nature*; Transcendental Club meets for first time; son Waldo born.

1837   Delivers address on "The American Scholar" to Phi Beta Kappa Society at Harvard; begins "Human Culture" lecture series in Boston.

1838   Delivers "Divinity School Address" at Harvard.

1839   Daughter Ellen Tucker Emerson born on February 24.

1840   Assists with first issue of the *Dial,* edited by Margaret Fuller.

1841   Publishes *Essays, First Series;* daughter Edith born on November 22; Henry David Thoreau moves into Emerson home as handyman; Brook Farm experiment begins.

1842   Son Waldo dies on January 27; assumes editorship of the *Dial.*

1843   Begins "New England" lecture series.

1844   Son Edward Waldo Emerson born on July 10; delivers first public address on slavery issue; publishes *Essays, Second Series.*

1845   Lectures on "Representative Men;" allows Thoreau to move into cabin at Walden Pond on Emerson property.

1846   Publishes first collection of poems.

1847-48 Makes second trip to Europe; lectures extensively while there.

1849   Publishes *Natures, Addresses, and Lectures.*

1850   Publishes *Representative Men;* makes first lecture tour to West; mourns drowning of Margaret Fuller.

1852   Speaks out on the Fugitive Slave Law; edits Margaret Fuller's memoirs.

1853   Mother Ruth Haskins Emerson dies at age eighty-five.

1854   Lectures extensively in the Midwest; Saturday Club meets first time; Thoreau publishes *Walden.*

1856   Publishes *English Traits.*

1859   Brother Robert Bulkeley dies on May 27.

1860   Publishes *The Conduct of Life.*

1862   Meets Abraham Lincoln; gives oration at funeral of Henry David Thoreau.

1863   Praises Lincoln's Emancipation Proclamation; Mary Moody Emerson (Aunt Mary) dies.

1866   Receives honorary doctorate at Harvard.

1867   Publishes *May-Day and Other Poems;* elected Harvard "overseer."

1868   Brother William Emerson dies on September 13.

1870   Publishes *Society and Solitude;* memory begins to fail.

1871   Makes trip to California; meets naturalist John Muir.

1872   Concord house burns on July 24; makes third trip to Europe; receives enthusiastic welcome on return home.

1874   Publishes *Parnassus.*

1875   Publishes *Letters and Social Aims,* edited by James Elliot Cabot; stops writing in journal.

1876   Gives last lecture at University of Virginia.

1881   Appears before public for last time at Massachusetts Historical Society upon death of Thomas Carlyle.

1881   Dies in Concord on April 27 at age seventy-eight; buried in Sleepy Hollow Cemetery.

Concord, 21 July
Mass.tts } 1855

Dear Sir,

I am not
blind to the worth of
the wonderful gift of
"Leaves of Grass." I find
it the most extraordina
piece of wit & wisdom
that america has yet
contributed. I am very

SOURCES

CHAPTER ONE: FAMILY TIES

p. 12,   "Mr. Puffer preached . . ." James Eliot Cabot, *A Memoir of Ralph Waldo Emerson* (Boston: Houghton, Mifflin and Company, 1887), 1:27.

p. 13,   "at the gate . . ." Ralph L. Rusk, *The Life of Ralph Waldo Emerson* (New York: Charles Scribner's Sons, 1949), 24.

p. 13,   "I remember sitting . . . " John McAleer, *Ralph Waldo Emerson: Days of Encounter* (Boston: Little, Brown and Company, 1984), 38.

p. 14,   "When I was a boy . . ." Ibid., 39.

p. 14,   "who twice or thrice . . ." Rusk, *The Life of Ralph Waldo Emerson,* 23.

p. 15,   "Ralph does not read . . ." Gay Wilson Allen, *Waldo Emerson* (New York: Penguin Books, 1981), 4.

p. 15,   "I feel daily . . ." Robert D. Richardson, Jr., *Emerson: The Mind on Fire* (Berkeley: University of California Press, 1995), 21.

p. 16,   "expressed himself . . ." Oliver Wendell Holmes, *Ralph Waldo Emerson-John Lothrop Motley-Two Memoirs* (Oliver Wendell Holmes, 1906; repr., West Press, 2007), 9.

A letter from Emerson to poet Walt Whitman, July 1855

p. 16-17,   "in his theological . . ." Ibid.

p. 17,   "Our family . . ." McAleer, *Ralph Waldo Emerson: Days of Encounter,* 23.

p. 18,   "Her mind and her . . ." Ibid., 23.

p. 18,   "rude speech . . .sooner or later," Ibid., 29.

p. 19,   "Your residence in my . . ." Rusk, *The Life of Ralph Waldo Emerson,* 24.

p. 19,   "kind aunt . . ." Frederic Ives Carpenter, *Emerson Handbook* (New York: Hendricks House, Inc., 1953), 4.

p. 19,   "high counsel . . ." McAleer, *Ralph Waldo Emerson: Days of Encounter,* 33.

p. 19,   "Lift your aims . . ." Ibid.

p. 20,   "had a peculiar . . ." Ibid., 20.

p. 22,   "punished for it . . ." Allen, *Waldo Emerson,* 25.

CHAPTER TWO: A DEVELOPING MIND

p. 25,   "How is it, Ralph . . ." McAleer, *Ralph Waldo Emerson,* 43.

p. 26,   "Fie on you! . . ." Rusk, *The Life of Ralph Waldo Emerson,* 52.

p. 26,   "A smile was on . . ." Allen, *Waldo Emerson,* 33.

p. 28,   "the regular course . . ." Rusk, *The Life of Ralph Waldo Emerson,* 60.

p. 29,   "to give me advice . . ." Allen, *Waldo Emerson,* 43.

p. 29,   "necessary to understand . . ." Rusk, *The Life of Ralph Waldo Emerson,* 68.

p. 30,   "It appears to me . . ." Cabot, *A Memoir of Ralph Waldo Emerson,* 68.

p. 31,   "one of the fifteen . . ." McAleer, *Ralph Waldo Emerson: Days of Encounter,* 59.

p. 32,   "the classic New England . . ." Allen, *Waldo Emerson,* 51.

p. 33,   "I find myself . . ." Ibid., 53-54.

p. 34,   "A chamber alone . . ." George Edward Woodberry, *Ralph Waldo Emerson* (New York: Macmillan Company, 1926), 16.

p. 34-35, "a goading sense . . ." Rusk, *The Life of Ralph Waldo Emerson,* 97.

p. 35,   "I was nineteen . . ." Allen, *Waldo Emerson,* 60.

p. 35,   "a moment's respite . . ." William H. Gilman et al., *The Journals and Miscellaneous Notebooks of Ralph Waldo Emerson* (Cambridge, MA: The Belknap Press, 1960), 46-47.

p. 36,   "I am seeking to put . . ." Cabot, *A Memoir of Ralph Waldo Emerson,* 96.

p. 36,   "GOOD-BYE, proud world! . . ." Ralph Waldo Emerson, *The Works of Ralph Waldo Emerson* (New York: Black's Readers Service Company, 1925), 12-13.

p. 38,   "Christianity is not . . ." Allen, *Waldo Emerson,* 64.

CHAPTER THREE: CALL TO MINISTRY

p. 41,   "I have closed . . ." Rusk, *The Life of Ralph Waldo Emerson,* 108.

p. 44,   "My years are passing . . ." William H. Gilman and Alfred R. Ferguson, eds., *The Journals and Miscellaneous Notebooks of Ralph Waldo Emerson* (Cambridge, MA: Belknap Press, 1963), 3:15.

p. 44,   "Have you seen . . ." Cabot, *A Memoir of Ralph Waldo Emerson,* 115.

p. 45,   "If they had examined . . ." George Willis Cooke, *Ralph Waldo Emerson: His Life, Writings and Philosophy* (Boston: James R. Osgood and Company, 1882), 24.

p. 45,   "Young man, you'll never . . ." Edward Waldo Emerson and Waldo Emerson Forbes, eds., *Journals of Ralph Waldo Emerson* (Boston: Houghton Mifflin Company, 1909), 2:98.

p. 45,   "the mouse in my . . ." McAleer, *Ralph Waldo Emerson,* 84.

p. 48,   "I am all clay . . ." Cabot, *A Memoir of Ralph Waldo Emerson,* 131.

p. 49,   "I am living . . ." Ralph L. Rusk, ed., *The Letters of Ralph Waldo Emerson* (New York: Columbia University Press, 1939), 1:227.

p. 50,   "I have little apprehension . . ." Cabot, *A Memoir of Ralph Waldo Emerson,* 141-142.

p. 51, "She is too lovely . . ." Allen, *Waldo Emerson,* 127.

p. 51, "it would still have been . . ." Henry F. Pommer, *Emerson's First Marriage* (Carbondale: Southern Illinois University Press, 1967), 13.

p. 53, "I like her better . . ." Ibid., 37.

p. 53, "There's an apprehension . . ." Cabot, *A Memoir of Ralph Waldo Emerson,* 147.

p. 53, "Providence presented you . . ." Cooke, *Ralph Waldo Emerson,* 27.

p. 54, "She spoke this afternoon . . ." McAleer, *Ralph Waldo Emerson,* 106-107.

p. 55, "My angel is gone . . ." Rusk, *The Letters of Ralph Waldo Emerson,* 318.

CHAPTER FOUR: COPING WITH ADVERSITIES

p. 57, "In looking back . . ." Cabot, *A Memoir of Ralph Waldo Emerson,* 153.

p. 59, "had met with men . . ." Ibid., 197.

p. 59-60, "A man contains all . . ." Ibid., 202-203.

p. 61, "I announce this fact . . ." Rusk, *The Letters of Ralph Waldo Emerson,* 436.

p. 63, "Now commences a new . . ." Cabot, *A Memoir of Ralph Waldo Emerson,* 272-273.

p. 64, "I now know all . . ." Richardson, *Emerson,* 236.

p. 64,   "a very accomplished . . ." Merton M. Sealts, Jr., ed., *The Journals and Miscellaneous Notebooks of Ralph Waldo Emerson* (Cambridge, MA: The Belknap Press, 1965), 5:188.

p. 65,   "Rhodora! if the sages . . ." Ralph Waldo Emerson, *The Works of Ralph Waldo Emerson: Four Volumes in One* (New York: Tudor Publishing Company, 1941), 13.

p. 65,   "very unsatisfactory . . ." Richardson, *Emerson,* 245.

p. 65,   "deeper and broader . . ." Ibid.

CHAPTER FIVE: THE PRIVATE INDIVIDUAL

p. 69,   "a leaf, a drop . . ." Emerson, *The Works of Ralph Waldo Emerson,* 541.

p. 70,   "Why should we grope . . ." Ibid., 527.

p. 70,   "the highest imaginative . . ." Cooke, *Ralph Waldo Emerson,* 43.

p. 70,   "it proves to us . . ." Ibid.

p. 70,   "Last night at 11 . . ." Sealts, *The Journals and Miscellaneous Notebooks of Ralph Waldo Emerson,* 234.

p. 70,   "in the self-same robe . . ." Rusk, *The Life of Ralph Waldo Emerson,* 251.

p. 71,   "from his central position . . ." Cooke, *Ralph Waldo Emerson,* 49.

p. 71,   "By the rude bridge . . ." Emerson, *The Works of Ralph Waldo Emerson,* 59.

. 72,   "Our day of dependence . . ." Ibid., 555.

. 72,   "one in which . . ." Ibid., 556.

. 72,   "The book, the college . . ." Ibid., 558.

. 72,   "meek young men . . ." Ibid.

. 72,   "the world is nothing . . ." Ibid., 567.

. 73,   "an event without . . ." Oliver Wendell Homes, *Ralph Waldo Emerson* (Boston: Houghton, Mifflin and Company, 1885), 107.

. 73,   "our intellectual Declaration . . ." McAleer, *Ralph Waldo Emerson,* 235.

. 73-74, "Wherever a man comes . . ." R. W. Emerson, *Miscellanies; Embracing Nature, Addresses, and Lectures* (Boston: James R. Osgood and Company, 1875), 139.

. 74,   "Alone in all history . . ." Ibid., 70.

. 74,   "His real object . . ." McAleer, *Ralph Waldo Emerson,* 255.

. 75,   "Lidian, who magnanimously . . ."Allen, *Waldo Emerson,* 336.

CHAPTER SIX: FLUX OF LIFE

. 77,   "Trust thyself: every . . ." Emerson, *The Works of Ralph Waldo Emerson,* 98.

. 77,   "Nothing is at last . . ." Ibid., 99.

. 77,   "What I must do . . ." Ibid., 100.

p. 77,   "For non-conformity . . ." Ibid., 101.

p. 78,   "A foolish consistency . . ." Ibid., 102.

p. 78,   "to be great . . ." Ibid.

p. 78,   "many single thoughts . . ." Rusk, *The Life of Ralph Waldo Emerson,* 284.

p. 78-79, "had not gone . . ." Ibid.

p. 82,   "My music makes . . ." McAleer, *Ralph Waldo Emerson,* 376.

p. 83,   "The South-wind brings . . ." Emerson, *The Works of Ralph Waldo Emerson,* 55.

p. 83,   "I wish I had . . ." McAleer, *Ralph Waldo Emerson,* 211-212.

p. 85,   "It is high time . . ." Ibid., 212.

p. 85,   "You may love . . . Joseph Slater, ed., *The Correspondence of Emerson and Carlyle* (New York: Columbia University Press, 1964), 320.

p. 88,   "Life is a train . . ." Emerson, *The Works of Ralph Waldo Emerson,* 226.

p. 89,   "we were to have . . ." Richardson, *Emerson,* 429.

p. 90,   "one of the most peculiar . . ." Rusk, *The Life of Ralph Waldo Emerson,* 322.

p. 91,   "hymns to the devil . . ." Allen, *Waldo Emerson,* 466.

p. 91,   "mines of rich . . ." Rusk, *The Life of Ralph Waldo Emerson,* 323.

CHAPTER SEVEN: TAKING A STAND

p. 96,   "The fairest American . . ." Warren Staebler, *Ralph Waldo Emerson* (New York: Twayne Publishers, Inc., 1973), 132.

p. 96,   "I will not obey . . ." Rusk, *The Life of Ralph Waldo Emerson,* 367.

p. 95, 96, "An immoral law . . ." Staebler, *Ralph Waldo Emerson,* 132.

p. 97-98, "After living with her . . ." Rusk, *The Letters of Ralph Waldo Emerson, IV,* 398.

p. 98,   "no better book . . ." Donald Yannella, *Ralph Waldo Emerson* (Boston: Twayne Publishers, 1982), 109.

p. 99,   "a true hero, but . . ." Rusk, *The Life of Ralph Waldo Emerson,* 401.

p. 100,   "Things are pretty . . ." Emerson, *The Works of Ralph Waldo Emerson,* 414-415.

p. 100,   "You have grown older . . ." Slater, *The Correspondence of Emerson and Carlyle,* 533-534.

p. 100,   "wants the fire . . ." Allen, *Waldo Emerson,* 605.

p. 100,   "sublime, the pronunciation . . ." Rusk, *The Life of Ralph Waldo Emerson,* 405.

p. 102,   "the fruit of other . . ." Allen, *Waldo Emerson,* 612.

CHAPTER EIGHT: SPIRIT UNBOUND

p. 105,   "To-day unbind the . . ." Emerson, *The Works of Ralph Waldo Emerson,* 80.

p. 106,   "Her genius was . . ." Rusk, *The Letters of Ralph Waldo Emerson, V,* 326.

p. 106,   "We meet under . . ." Richardson, *Emerson,* 553.

p. 106,   "Rarely was a man . . ." Rusk, *The Life of Ralph Waldo Emerson,* 427.

p. 106,   "This event has brought . . ." Rusk, *The Letters of Ralph Waldo Emerson, V,* 408-409.

p. 107,   "It is time . . ." Emerson, *The Works of Ralph Waldo Emerson: Four Volumes in One,* 289.

p. 111,   "House/burned . . ." Ronald A. Bosco and Glen M. Johnson, eds., *The Journals and Miscellaneous Notebooks of Ralph Waldo Emerson,* (Cambridge, MA: The Belknap Press, 1982), 16:278.

p. 111,   "When nature indicates . . ." Rusk, *The Life of Ralph Waldo Emerson,* 454.

p. 112,   "Yesterday I . . ." Cabot, *A Memoir of Ralph Waldo Emerson, II,* 658.

p. 112,   "this trick of sympathy . . ." McAleer, *Ralph Waldo Emerson,* 625.

p. 113,   "I have reached an . . ." Ibid., 629.

p. 114,   "The passive Master . . ." Emerson, *The Works of Ralph Waldo Emerson: Four Volumes in One,* 90.

Emerson's study

BIBLIOGRAPHY

Allen, Gay Wilson. *Waldo Emerson.* New York: Penguin Books, 1981.

Bosco, Ronald A., and Glen M. Johnson, eds. *The Journals and Miscellaneous Notebooks of Ralph Waldo Emerson. Vol. 16.* Cambridge, MA: The Belknap Press, 1982.

Cabot, James Eliot. *A Memoir of Ralph Waldo Emerson. 2 vols.* Boston: Houghton, Mifflin and Company, 1887.

Carpenter, Frederic Ives. *Emerson Handbook.* New York: Hendricks House, Inc., 1953.

Coogan, Michael D., ed. *The New Oxford Annotated Bible.* New York: Oxford University Press, 2001.

Cooke, George Willis. *Ralph Waldo Emerson: His Life, Writings and Philosophy.* Boston: James R. Osgood and Company, 1882.

Emerson, Edward Waldo, and Waldo Emerson Forbes, eds. *Journals of Ralph Waldo Emerson. Vol. 2.* Boston: Houghton Mifflin Company, 1909.

Emerson, Ralph Waldo. *The Works of Ralph Waldo Emerson: Four Volumes in One.* New York: Tudor Publishing Company, 1941.

———. *The Works of Ralph Waldo Emerson.* New York: Black's Readers Service Company, 1925.

————. *Miscellanies; Embracing Nature, Addresses, and Lectures.* Boston: James R. Osgood and Company, 1875.

Ferguson, Alfred R., ed. *The Collected Works of Ralph Waldo Emerson: Nature, Addresses and Lectures.* Vol. 1. Cambridge, MA: The Belknap Press, 1971.

Firkens, O. W. *Ralph Waldo Emerson.* Mineola, NY: Dover Publications, Inc., 1915.

Gilman, William H., and Alfred R. Ferguson, eds. *The Journals and Miscellaneous Notebooks of Ralph Waldo Emerson.* Vol. 3. Cambridge, MA: The Belknap Press, 1963.

Gilman, William H. et al. *The Journals and Miscellaneous Notebooks of Ralph Waldo Emerson.* Cambridge, MA: The Belknap Press, 1960.

Holmes, Oliver Wendell. *Ralph Waldo Emerson.* Boston: Houghton, Mifflin and Company, 1885.

McAleer, John. *Ralph Waldo Emerson: Days of Encounter.* Boston: Little, Brown and Company, 1984.

McGiffert, Arthur Cushman, Jr., ed. *Young Emerson Speaks.* Boston: Houghton Mifflin Company, 1938.

Plumstead, A. W., and Harrison Hayford, eds. *The Journals and Miscellaneous Notebooks of Ralph Waldo Emerson. Vol. VII: 1838-1842.* Cambridge, MA: The Belknap Press, 1969.

Pommer, Henry F. *Emerson's First Marriage.* Carbondale: Southern Illinois University Press, 1967.

Richardson, Robert D., Jr. *Emerson: The Mind on Fire.* Berkeley: University of California Press, 1995.

Rusk, Ralph L., ed. *The Letters of Ralph Waldo Emerson.*
Vol. 3. New York: Columbia University Press, 1939.

———. *The Life of Ralph Waldo Emerson.* New York: Charles
Scribner's Sons, 1949.

Sealts, Merton M., Jr., ed. *The Journals and Miscellaneous Notebooks of Ralph Waldo Emerson. Vol. 5.* Cambridge, MA: The
Belknap Press, 1965.

Slater, Joseph, ed. *The Correspondence of Emerson and Carlyle.*
New York: Columbia University Press, 1964.

Staebler, Warren. *Ralph Waldo Emerson.* New York: Twayne Publishers, Inc., 1973.

Woodberry, George Edward. *Ralph Waldo Emerson.* New York:
The Macmillan Company, 1926.

Yannella, Donald. *Ralph Waldo Emerson.* Boston: Twayne Publishers, 1982.

WEB SITES

http://www.pbs.org/wnet/ihas/poet/emerson.html

A short biography of Emerson, along with excerpts from some of his writings are featured on this PBS online site.

http://quod.lib.umich.edu/e/emerson/

Thanks to the University of Michigan, visitors to this site will find a digital edition of the *Complete Works of Ralph Waldo Emerson,* Centenary Edition, edited and with notes by Edward Waldo Emerson.

http://www.emersonsermons.com/

The sermons preached by Ralph Waldo Emerson during his years as a Unitarian minister (1826-39) are provided here by the American Unitarian Conference. The Web site also has links to a biographical sketch, several articles, and the Ralph Waldo Emerson Society.

Ralph Waldo Emerson's father was the minister of this church in its original location in Chauncey Place. This is the current Unitarian Church at the corner of Marlborough and Berkeley Streets in Boston. This is a photo from the early 1900s in the Robert N. Dennis collection of stereoscopic views.

Self-

INDEX

Alcott, Bronson, 66, *66,* 76, 80, 85–86, *86,* 113
American Revolutionary War, 22, *70,* 71, *103*

Battle of Lexington, 71
Boston Public Latin School, 20, 23, 26, 28, 29
Brook Farm, 66, 80, 97
Brown, John, 98–99, *99*
Brownson, Orestes, 66, 74, 91

Calvin, John, 38
Carlyle, Thomas, 54, 58–59, *59,* 85, 93, 100, 112–113
Channing, Edward Tyrrel, 32–33
Channing, William Ellery, 32, 37–38
Civil War, 99, *99,* 100, 102, *103*
Clarke, James, 66
Clay, Henry, 95
Coleridge, Samuel Taylor, 54, 58, *59*
Concord, Massachusetts, 19, *19,* 23, 25, 62, 71, 112
Concord Social Library, 62, 87

Dial, The, 75–76, *75,* 84, 85, 94
Douglas, Stephen Arnold, 95, *96*

Emancipation Proclamation, 102–103, 105
Emerson, Charles (brother), 18, 44–45, 51, 53–54, 63

Emerson, Edward Bliss (brother), 18, 26–27, 37, 43–44, 46, 49–50, 53, 61, 95, 106
Emerson, Edward Waldo (son), 84, *84,* 100, 102–103, 112–113
Emerson, Ellen (daughter), 75, 82–83, 89, 100, 107, 109, 111–112
Emerson, Ellen Tucker (first wife), 49–55, 57, 61, 75, 98
Emerson, John Clarke (brother), 15
Emerson, Lidian Jackson (second wife), 61–63, 70, 73, 75, 81, 83–85, *84,* 89, 93, 102, 109, 111–113
Emerson, Mary Caroline (sister), 17–18, 23
Emerson, Mary Moody (aunt), 17–20, 26, 35–36, 45, 52–54, 58, 61, 63, 74, 78, 98, 106
Emerson, Ralph Waldo, *10, 12, 116, 134*
character, 25–26, 42
childhood, 12–15, 17–20, 23, 25–26
controversies, 74–75
courtship, 50–53
death, 113–114
at divinity school, 41–42, 44, 49
education, 15, 20–22, 26–28
essays, 59, 87–88, 99–100, 109
and ethics, 96–97
family issues, 43–44, 49, 63, 106

PHOTO CREDITS

Cover: Private Collection
10: Courtesy of Library of Congress
11: Used under license from istockphoto.com
12: Courtesy of the Concord Free Public Library
13: Used under license from istockphoto.com
14: Used under license from istockphoto.com
15: Used under license from istockphoto.com
17: Used under license from istockphoto.com
19: Used under license from istockphoto.com
20: Used under license from istockphoto.com
21: Courtesy of Library of Congress
22: Courtesy of Library of Congress
24: Used under license from istockphoto.com
25: Used under license from istockphoto.com
26: Used under license from istockphoto.com
27: Used under license from istockphoto.com
28: Used under license from istockphoto.com
31: Used under license from istockphoto.com
35: Private Collection
38: Used under license from istockphoto.com
40: Used under license from istockphoto.com
43: Used under license from istockphoto.com
46: Used under license from istockphoto.com
49: Used under license from istockphoto.com
50: Used under license from istockphoto.com
52: Used under license from istockphoto.com
55: Used under license from istockphoto.com
56: Used under license from istockphoto.com
59: Top image: Courtesy of the National Portrait Gallery; middle image,
Courtesy of The Art Institute of Chicago; bottom image, Courtesy of
the University of Texas Libraries, The University of Texas at Austin
60: Private Collection

62: Used under license from istockphoto.com
64: Private Collection
65: Used under license from istockphoto.com
66: Private Collection
68: Used under license from istockphoto.com
71: Private Collection
73: Private Collection
75: Private Collection
77: Used under license from istockphoto.com
78: Used under license from istockphoto.com
80: Courtesy of Library of Congress
81: Used under license from istockphoto.com
82: Used under license from istockphoto.com
84: Courtesy of New York Public Library
86: Private Collection
87: Private Collection
78: Used under license from istockphoto.com
88: Courtesy of Library of Congress
91: Used under license from istockphoto.com
92: Used under license from istockphoto.com
96: Courtesy of Library of Congress
99: Courtesy of the U.S. Military, U.S. National Archives
and Records Adminstration
100: Courtesy of Library of Congress
103: Courtesy of Library of Congress
104: Used under license from istockphoto.com
107: Used under license from istockphoto.com
108: Courtesy of Library of Congress
110: Used under license from istockphoto.com
113: Used under license from istockphoto.com
114: Private Collection
116: Courtesy of Library of Congress
120: Used under license from istockphoto.com
122: Courtesy of Library of Congress
133: Used under license from istockphoto.com
134: Courtesy of Library of Congress
138: Courtesy of the New York Public Library